AFRICANITY AND THE BLACK FAMILY

The Development of a Theoretical Model

1985
A BLACK FAMILY INSTITUTE PUBLICATION
P. O. BOX 24739
Oakland, California 94623

ISBN 0-939205-01-7

CONTENTS

Foreword:

The scholarship and work of the Institute's scholars and associates are published for wider distribution under the auspices of the Development and Dissemination Division's Black Family Institute Publications. We are especially pleased to publish, *Africanity and The Black Family: The Development of a Theoretical Model* by Wade W. Nobles.

For the first time in a single place, the seminal theoretical thinking of Dr. Nobles is put forth for our examination and benefit. Not only does *Africanity and the Black Family: The Development of a Theoretical Model*, provide the student of the Black family with a framework for critiquing the field of Black family scholarship, it constructs a unique model for engaging in authentic scientific inquiry from an Afrocentric perspective and demonstrates with original research the application and implications of an Afrocentric theoretical and empirical framework for the examination of Black family life.

This book will clearly serve as another tool in the arsenal of instruments needed for the development of an Afrocentric science. It will, without question, help to guide and fortify the Afrocentric thrust in Black family studies.

i

As such, The Institute's Development and Dissemination Division is especially pleased to share this text with a wider audience of students and scholars.

William E. Cavil, III
Associate Director
Development and Dissemination

Acknowledgments:

The theoretical model discussed in this text is the result of over a decade of applied research in the African-American community as well as considerable first-hand experience studying African, Caribbean and African-American culture, value systems, and lifestyles. In effect, *Africanity and the Black Family: The Development of a Theoretical Model* is grounded in the experience of one thinker living and studying the "African way" as reflected in African-American family life. Like all the work conducted at the Institute, this text is the result of the collective genius of all African peoples filtered through those few of us who struggle to establish an Afrocentric authority for things dealing with African people.

In completing the text this author is indebted to all the sources of Black genius, especially those at the Institute, who have shaped and corrected the thinking reflected in this work. In so doing, I acknowledge that if this text has value, then the credit belongs to them and to the most High. If there is any flaw in this text it must be charged to my personal inability to translate the collective genius of African and African-American people.

In Chapter 1 the role of "criticism" and the need for "creativity" in science is explicated as an introduction to theoretical development. Chapter 2 follows this discussion with a brief overview of the legacy and intellectual pitfalls of non-Black research and scholarship. In developing an orientation for scientific inquiry,

Chapter 3 identifies several theoretical notions and empirical considerations critical to the process of intellectually examining and defining Black families. In Chapter 4 the epistemological problems associated with analyzing the Black family are discussed and the concepts of "transubstantiation" and "conceptual incarceration" are offered as methods for guaranteeing the validity of Black family research. Chapter 5 offers in some detail the necessity for utilizing African culture as the basis for understanding African-American families, while Chapter 6 provides an outline of the structural features of the Africanity model. In addition to the concluding chapter which provides examples of several clear applications of the Africanity model, this text also offers a glossary of terms and concepts critical to the understanding and utilization of an Afrocentric framework.

Wade W. Nobles

CHAPTER ONE

CRITICISM AND CREATIVITY: AN INTRODUCTION TO THEORETICAL DEVELOPMENT

Chapter 1

Criticism and Creativity:
An Introduction to Theoretical
Development

It is general knowledge for those who have examined the research literature on the Black family, that for well over three-quarters of a century the issue of Black family life has been a subject of scientific investigation. It is also equally known that during this period, the examiners of Black family life have consistently offered scientific "evidence", "information", "theory" and "analyses" which focused on the so-called "problems" inherent in Black family systems or which, in their conclusion, verified that the Black family system was an organization inherently laden with problems and inadequacies. Before discussing these conditions, I should point out, parenthetically, that the argument to follow does not support the conclusion that Black family life in America is absent of problems. The obvious fact is that being Black in a White, racist society is problematic by definition. The family life of Black people can be, and is, characterized by real and definite problems associated with racism and oppression. To recognize this while simultaneously calling into question the historical character of the research literature which overwhelmingly defines Black family life in negativistic, problem-laden, pathological terms is not inconsistent. To the contrary, to call into question the traditional work on the Black family while simultaneously recognizing that there are real problems associated with and reflected in Black family life, is to recognize the complex nature of the phenomenon and the inability of the traditional research models to accurately assess the reality of Black family life.

As noted in the text, *"Understanding the Black Family"* (Nobles & Goddard,1984), the late 1960's witnessed more and more Black scholars seeing the need to be critical of the treatment of Blacks in the social sciences (cf. Billingsley, 1968; Hill, 1972; Ladner,1972; Staples, 1971). The history of the "negative" study of the Black family is indeed interesting in recognition of the thesis that the nature of a society influences the kind of knowledge to which its people are exposed (Mannheim, 1936). The apparent epistemological dilemma is more succinctly recognized in Kuhn's (1963) teachings. He notes that man is always limited in what he can know, by what he does know, even though he may not know what he knows.

In recognition of the social relativity of information concerning the Black family, Staples (1971) argues that the imposition of ethnocentric (White) values on the analysis of Black family life precludes the application of much, if not most, of the previous and current research and theory concerning the Black family. In his discussion of "The Black Family

Revisited" (1974), Professor Staples' critical analysis of the major orientations historically characterizing the research on Black families illustrates the problems imbedded in non-Black scholarship. Similarly, it has also been noted (Nobles, 1976b) that having accepted the "time" and "space" limitations of White social reality as well as the consistent definitions within those time and space references, American scholarship and research on the Black family has been bound only to an analysis of the existential development of Black family life in America. That is to say, the study of the Black family has been primarily a comparative analysis of Black family experiences and White family experiences.

Unfortunately, in comparing the Black family to the reality of White families, invariably the Black family has been viewed as the White family's "illegitimate soul-brother". The consequence of this false comparison has been the depiction of the Black family as a dark-skinned White family which is disorganized, pathological, victimized, and/or impoverished. In accepting the White family as the standard family or "conceptual family", researchers and their research on the Black family have been inextricably bound to an inappropriate comparative model and locked into an inaccurate analytical framework. Not only is this the epitome of conceptually incarcerated research, but we also recognize this depiction of the Black family as an illegitimate White family, to be a misconception and unscientific.

A primary concern for this discussion is ultimately to offer a theoretical framework for critiquing the literature on the Black family which therefore will provide us with a systematic way to refute theoretically and empirically the erroneous and destructive conceptualizations of Black family life found in the literature and to suggest the initial guidelines for guaranteeing an accurate and authentic characterization of the Black family. As a general background to the objectives of this discussion, it must be pointed out that some scholars are ready to contend that the what, how and why of Black scholarship will be judged by history as a paradigmatic shift in the social sciences. In agreement with this perspective, it is further suggested that Black research on the Black family will be seen as a shift from an a priori pathological paradigm to a more accurate and representational one. In this regard, it is believed that the paradigmatic shift in Black family research will be more than just a shift in perspective. Over the last twenty years the Black family research done by Blacks has gone virtually unnoticed, and yet all indicators seem to suggest that the research programmes of the 60's, 70's and 80's are providing an altogether different picture of the Black family as well as forcing revisions and modifications in the fields of social science in general. Unfortunately, there has not been an exclusive and comprehensive review and analysis of this important shift in the social sciences. In recognizing that human development and human relations are, in part, governed by the ideas which dictate what is normal and/or appropriate, the ultimate rationale for this text is in the potential it has for aiding us in understanding (1) the relationship between Black family life and the development of human beings; and (2) the way in which information and ideas about our institutions (i.e. the Black family) impact on the ability of scientists to understand those institutions. Accordingly, in providing an alternative theoretical framework for the analysis of the Black family, one simultaneously provides a tool for exposing the value and/or utility (or lack thereof) of the ideas which purport to shape our understanding of Black reality. It is, consequently, through our ability to critique and refute destructive and erroneous ideas that we are able to defend ourselves from the behavior and conditions which are the consequences of those ideas. Similarly, it is through our ability to create and develop ideas conducive to our own growth and development that we are able to reinforce those behaviors and conditions which affirm and protect our well being. Hence, the value of this work is directly embedded in its ability to, in part, assist in the development of a perspective and attitude of "criticism and creativity" which is requisite to the development of authentic and accurate information and ideas about Black family life.

CHAPTER TWO

THE LEGACY OF NON-BLACK RESEARCH

Chapter 2

The Legacy of Non-Black Research

In his discussion of the distinction between Black studies and the study of Black people (cf: Clark, 1972), Professor X (Clark) makes a cogent argument for the critical relationship between the interpretive framework in scientific studies and the validity of the information acquired in such investigation. The position taken by Professor X (Clark) is that one's ability to understand Black reality is limited if the "interpretive framework" for the analysis of that reality is based on assumptions associated with non-Black reality.

The scientific orientations used in the study of Black families have essentially been established on interpretive or conceptual frameworks based in an understanding of, and perception about, non-Black reality. The primary orientations (poverty-acculturation, pathological, and victimization) fall into this category and will exemplify this point. The poverty-acculturated studies (cf: Frazier, 1932; Bernard, 1966; Jeffers, 1967; Chilman, 1966), for example, argued that Black people, upon being thrust into bondage, lost whatever cultural stability they had as Africans. These studies of Black family life focused, therefore, on economic conditions of the Black population, which were supposedly the cause of Black family disorganization. The pathologically-oriented studies (cf: Moynihan, 1965; Bernard, 1966; Aldous, 1969; Rainwater, 1970) argued that in relationship to the family, there, in fact, existed no civilized and/or cultural stability in African life. Hence, the heritage of Black family life was one of savagery and barbarism. Consequently, the study of Black family life here focused on the supposedly negative structural and functional features in Black families, which led to poverty, ignorance and crime. The victim-oriented studies (cf: Rodman, 1963; Liebow, 1967; Willie, 1970; Scanzoni, 1970) argued that Black families would be just like White families if Black people were not the victims of job discrimination and educational inequality. Here, the study of Black family life focused on demonstrating that the perceived differences in Black and White families were due to economic and educational differences.

The assertion characterizing or common to all three of these orientations are that Black families or the Black family phenomenon is "made in America". That is to say, there is a homogeneous American culture and, consequently, families in American society should have a common definition. The fact that the condition of Black family life is different from the conceptual character of White American family life leads to the conclusion that the differences perceived in Black families represented a deviation from the "normative" family. Hence, the Black family was perceived as a deviant version of American family organization.

✳ The interpretive framework for such an analysis was naturally the White family system. By assuming a common cultural reality between Blacks and Whites, one accepts a common singular theoretical framework for interpreting their respective lifestyles. Cultural homogeneity is the first lie. In accepting this lie as true, research on the Black family has had to reconcile the real differences between these two family types and the belief that they should not be different. The reconciliation of the perceived differences between Black and White families was the creation of the notion of Black family deviancy. The second falsification associated with these orientations to the study of Black families was, in fact, that "difference", by definition means "deviant". Couple the deviant assertion with White racism and the results appear in a manner which a priority defines the White family as "normative" and the Black family as "deviant". Racist models coupled with shabby, unsophisticated scientific treatment (from conceptualization to interpretation) of Black family life is the legacy contemporary researchers struggle with, and are confused by, in the current analyses of Black family life.

The best example of the burden of this legacy and the confusion caused by it is revealed by Hare (1976). In discussing "what Black intellectuals misunderstand about the Black family", Dr. Hare reveals the real socio-political aspects of research on the Black family. He notes, for instance, that in 1963 the American Academy of Arts and Sciences, as a result of "private conversations", issued invitations to twenty-four "eminent" authors to attend a closed conference at the House of the American Academy of Arts and Sciences. The invitation to what was later to be called the 1964 Planning Group, came with instructions to interrupt whatever personal work they were about in order to devote the next full year to a study of the Negro American. Dr. Hare notes in this discussion that Whites outnumbered Blacks on this planning group three to one and that the members (1) of the group held in common a belief that integration was the preferred approach to Black protest and, by implication, the solution to "the Black problem".

As a direct result of the work of this group, two volumes of DAEDALUS, the Academy's official publication, were published, later to be followed by the Talcott Parsons and Kenneth Clark edited text, THE NEGRO AMERICAN (1967).

More important than these published works, however, is the role White social theoreticians played in influencing the direction of Black family research. Hare notes, for instance, that Moynihan's controversial U.S. Department of Labor report on "The Negro Family: The Case For National Action" took final form during his involvement with the group. However, more significant than Moynihan's contribution is the fact that Moynihan's Harvard colleagues, Erik Erikson, a psychoanalyst, and Talcott Parsons, a sociological theorist, expressed an interest or desire for Black intellectuals to begin to emphasize the "positives" rather than the "negatives" in the study of the Black family. It is true that during the next few years, several studies were undertaken in the vein of "positive" research on the Black family; and, even though Billingsley (1968) openly acknowledges an indebtedness to Talcott Parsons, it is not clear that those identified as adherents (2) to the "strengths of Black families" approach would consider themselves belonging to that school. Nevertheless, Nathan Hare suggests that "Erik Erikson drew the explicit blueprint and Talcott Parsons served as the master designer for the strength-of-Black-families school, which they left as a legacy for Black family research".

In taking up this orientation, Hare further argues that Black intellectuals adopted a theoretical approach which misdirected the analysis of Black family life and drew attention away from analyzing the "heinous conditions" imposed on Black families by an oppressive and racist society. Although Dr. Hare's discussion is very critical of the "strengths-of-Black-families" school, he unfortunately only identifies one of the debilitating aspects of this approach. He correctly noted that this legacy misdirected the Black scholars' attention from the societal factors influencing Black family life. He failed, however, to recognize that the other debilitating aspect of the planning group's guidance is that it disallowed the examination of Black families with an analytical framework based on the nature or "sensory" system of Black people. While we are in general agreement with Dr. Hare's revealing discussion, it, unfortunately, doesn't carry the critique far enough. It has to be noted, for instance, that by calling for an emphasis on the strengths of Black families, the planning group placed the inquiry at a level which didn't allow for an investigation of what constituted "strengths" given the socio-political, psycho-cultural realities of Black people. Once again, as with the negativistic research, the "positive" oriented research accepted, a priority, the meaning of "positive" as seen and defined by the dominant society. Dr. Hare alludes to this epistemological trap when he notes that from the position of the oppressed, one could argue that there are no true positives for an oppressed race under subjugated circumstances.

The debilitating aspect of the legacy is that the uncritical adoption of non-Black interpretive or analytical frameworks results in (1) mis-directing the analyses of Black family life, and (2) erroneously accepting alien assumptions and "meanings" which define the phenomena under investigation.

In order to break away from this legacy, one has to start with the latter point and move to the former. By proceeding in such a manner, it is believed that the stage for defining Black families will be set and ready for the drama of establishing an empirical and theoretical framework for the study of Black family life -- a framework which will be consistent with the socio-political and psycho-cultural realities of Black people.

Science and the Study of Black Family life:

What is important to address in this discussion is (1) the recognition of the connection between science and ideology and (2) the roots of Black intellectual thought regarding the understanding of Black reality-particularly the Black family.

The connection between science and ideology is, of course, obvious even if it is seldom made explicit. Ideology is essentially an instrument which provides a critique of reality and thereby influences the nature of the consciousness (awareness). As such, ideology defines and guides appropriate behavior or action, and serves to refine and raise the level of practice (cf: Karenga, 1978). Science is nothing more than a set of ideas -- representing reality. It is, in fact, no more than a formal reconstruction of a people's reality. Since ideology serves to influence a people's awareness of their reality, science, particularly social science, must incorporate in its reconstruction the prevailing ideological position of its creators. It is extremely important to recognize that the ideas of science and the interest of science, and even the definition of science, are bound in the time and historical condition of the society in which its developers live. The ideas of science do not develop in empty space, or even abstract space where there is supposedly nothing but ideas. The ideas, interests, application and definition of science go on in a human world; and, human life is social. There is, therefore, no science which is not in some part a "social" science. Similarly, when the social reality is defined by racism and oppression, or in a society which depends on racism and oppression, there can be no science which is not, in part, oppressive and racist.

It is obvious or should be that racism is an ideology in this country. Just as science and technology have gone hand and hand in the last three hundred years to assist in the development of the western world[3]; so, too, has the application of "science" to the understanding and definition of the human (social) condition served to maintain the social reality of racism.   In effect, a proper understanding of Black intellectual thinking must, in fact, be explained by understanding the impact that a racist environment had on our ability to grasp and understand, on an intellectual level, Black reality. The connection between science as a reconstruction of reality and ideology as an instrument which influences the awareness of reality resulted in a real epistemological dilemma for Black thinkers; a dilemma which forced the Black pursuit of scientific analyses to be crippled by the prevailing definition and meaning of "science".

It is important to note that the science-ideology connection really clarified itself around the issue and "meaning" of the African for Whites. At the same time the development of Black intellectual thought was inspired by the need to understand the human condition of Black people while being imbedded in an intellectual atmosphere which 'ideologically' and 'scientifically' denied the humaneness of the African.

Historically, the response of Black intellectuals toward this dilemma has been to react to it in three distinct ways. Interestingly enough, the core focus of the Black reaction and intellectual development was also the meaning and definition of the African. It is necessary to note here that early Black intellectual thought (unlike today's) centered on the issue of the condition and development

of the Black man. With such a focus, it is not
surprising that early Black intellectual thinking
took form and was most clearly manifested in
the political arena under the banner of
nationalism. Understand, however, that the
root of this political nationalism was the same
humane concern for the identification,
definition and creation of a condition which
would allow for the affirmation and
development of the new world African. Hence,
an analysis of the early intellectual thinking
around the question of nationalism reveals
particular insight into the development of
Black intellectual thought in general.

Turner (1920) suggests that in seeking to
define a condition which would allow Blacks to
grow and develop, early thinkers began to
consider the logic of what has come to be
known as the "back-to-Africa" movement.
Black involvement in this movement, however,
clearly reflected a deep concern for the
identity,definition, growth and development of
the Black man in the new world. Early Black
involvement with this movement, according to
Turner, can be analyzed in terms of a "pull-
push syndrome". The "push" effect, which led
to Black involvement, resulted from the
hostile, negativistic social, political and
economic climate of American racist ideology.
The "pull" effect, which also led to Black
involvement, resulted from an attraction to
Africa itself. The essence of Turner's argument
is that some Blacks got involved with the Back-
To-Africa movement because the nature of
America **pushed** them away, while others did
so because they were **pulled** to Africa. A
similar analogy can be made regarding Black

intellectual thought.

It is probably more accurate to suggest that participation and the reason for participating in the movement were behavioral expressions of an intellectual analysis of new world Blacks and their condition; intellectual analyses which are influenced by the "push" of America and the "pull" of Africa.

It is the centrality of Africa and its meaning to Black intellectual thought that I now wish to turn my attention. It seems evident that Africa, as a central theme in Black intellectual analyses, has resulted from both the "push" and the "pull" conditions. It is, however, the removal of Africa as the central framework in Black analyses which has, in my mind, resulted in the paralysis of Black thought. Hence, in terms of understanding Black reality, one could divide Black intellectual thinking into three categories: the pushed, the pulled and the paralyzed.

The Push, Pull and Paralysis of Black Thought

It is important to note that such divisions are dangerous and dysfunctional unless one notes that in each case the impetus for serious thinking regarding the condition of Black people was due to a genuine and earnest regard for one's people, and as such, reflects the common underlying humaneness of the Black thinkers found in each category. With this in mind, I will try to exemplify the centrality of Africa on the subsequent push, pull and paralysis of Black thought. One can argue that early Black thinking was clearly more ideological; however, it is more accurate to recognize that in earlier periods of history intellectuals were less sophisticated in masking the merger between science and ideology.

Though most Black intellectuals were simultaneously pushed, pulled and paralyzed, for the purpose of this analysis I would like to focus on three individuals and discuss them as exclusive examples. As noted above, Black intellectual thought was to develop in an atmosphere which ideologically and scientifically defined the African as inferior, and implicitly and explicitly denied the central humaneness of his being. It was in this environment that the African had to address the issue of defining what conditions would be conducive to his psychological and physical development and well-being. In raising such a question, early Black thinkers had to openly address the issues of identity, "Blackness", "ideology", as well as to isolate the core problem and correct solution central to each.

In terms of the definition of Blackness, both the "pushed" and the "pulled" arrived at the same conclusion that African Blacks were a unique people unto themselves. Martin Delany, whom I offer as an example of the "pushed", spoke of the cultural uniqueness of African Blacks as a notion within a notion. He suggested or recognized that the Black race was endowed with natural properties allowing us to adapt to any climate. In terms of identity, however, Delany argued that we were Americans. He noted that...

"Our country is the United States. Here we were born, raised and educated; here are the scenes of our childhood...and the sacred graves of our devoted fathers and mothers and from here will we not be driven by any policy that

may be schemed against us".

In contrast and as an example of the "pulled", Edward Wilmont Blyden also recognized the uniqueness of Black people and strongly argued for the necessity of preserving the unique characteristics of African people. He asserted that we were Africans. Blyden stated that the Africans were a great race...

"...great in its vitality, in its powers of endurance and its prospects of perpetuity. It has passed through the fiery furnace of centuries of indigenous barbarism and foreign slavery and yet it remains unconsumed...It is sad to think that there are some Africans, especially among those who have enjoyed the advantages of foreign training, who are blind enough to the radical facts of humanity as to say, let us do away with the sentiment of race. Let us do away with our African personality and be lost, if possible, in another race".

Blyden believed that we could find the soul of the race through the careful study and appreciation of African customs and institutions. He, like Delany, felt that the erosion of the uniqueness of the African was central to the question of our development and well-being. However, Blyden felt that Christianity, which focused on changing African values, had a disruptive influence on Africans; while Delany contended that, as an oppressed people, "we have been deprived of our purity and corrupted in our native characteristics".

An analysis of Delany's writing suggests that he openly felt that America's rejection of his Blackness was the source of the Black man's problems and that if this country could cure itself of the disease of racism, the New World African could find an environment which would affirm and nourish his natural potential. Blyden's writing, however, suggests that he felt that Africa as a Black nation was the only condition conducive to the affirmation of the natural potential of New World Blacks. In the example of Delany, Black intellectual thought focused on the "external conditions" of America and concluded that America was not good for the New World Black man (ergo, the "pushed"). Black intellectual thought as exemplified by Blyden, however, focused on the "internal nature" of the African and concluded that Africa was good for the New World Black (ergo, the "pulled").

At this point it is somewhat obvious that the intellectual thinking of both these men was indeed influenced by, in one case, Delany's, the push of America; and, in the other, Blyden's, the pull of Africa. In the extreme case, the "pushed" felt that America and the meaning of America had mistakenly rejected them. Consequently, they have historically and consistently given America another chance, or more accurately, accepted every new chance to prove themselves American. In the extreme case, the "pulled" saw nothing good in America and have historically sought meaning outside of the definition of America. When the Civil War broke out, for instance, Delany (the "pushed") saw it as a "symbol of hope" for significant social change; and, in order to destroy the confederacy and thereby correct the source of Black people's mistaken rejection, he joined the Union army and put aside his dreams of a Black nation. Blyden (the "pulled") , however, argued that the Civil War had little meaning for Blacks. He stated that half the time spent in struggling against caste, if directed toward nationalism, would produce results immediately more useful and satisfying than curing America of her ills.

Even though the intellectual tradition characterized by Delany was significantly influenced by the push of America and that of Blyden by the pull of Africa, what is important to recognize is that both these traditions recognized the uniqueness of the African and struggled to establish a condition which would allow for the affirmation of that uniqueness. In both cases, Africa and its meaning was central to the expression of Black intellectual thought.

However, the intellectual environment in which Black thought was imbedded ultimately took its toll, and the prophetic fear of Blyden that Black thinkers would seek to "do away with our African personality and become lost in another race" emerged as the characteristic condition or quality of later Black thinking. This trend, we believe, came about as the consequence of removing Africa from its position of centrality. The placement of Africa as a tangential concern, if a concern at all, resulted in Black thought adopting the same central framework and focus that characterized traditional intellectual thinking in the United States (i.e. racism). A situation which resulted in our thinking being lost in the thinking of another race or what we have defined as conceptual incarceration or for this discussion, the paralysis of Black thought.

An example of this paralysis can be found in the seminal work of E. Franklin Frazier.

Though full of analytical contradictions, Frazier strongly argued that as a consequence of slavery Black people had been stripped of their traditional social and cultural heritage (Frazier, 1939). In terms of sexual behavior, for example, he argued that the sexual behavior of "negroes", like the sexual behavior of peoples all over the world, should be studied in relation to the social and cultural context in which the attitudes and patterns of behavior regarding sex are formed (cf. Frazier, 1939: p.109). He noted, for instance, that in Africa, sexual behavior is rigorously regulated by customs and mores of the different African societies. However, as a result of European contact, social disorganization resulted in unregulated sexual relationships and what might be regarded as immoral sexual conduct. He rightfully pointed out that, even with this new complexity added to African human processes, sexual conduct can only be viewed as immoral from the standpoint of the traditional African norms (and not European) governing sexual behavior. Because he accepted the assumption, however, of the destruction of African culture and heritage in the case of Black American slaves, he argued that the sexual behavior of Black Americans presented a different problem. For Frazier, the issue of Black American sexuality was one wherein *"we are dealing with a people who have been stripped of their traditional social and cultural heritage and who have been in the process of assimilating European culture over a period of three centuries or more"*. After reviewing the impact of slavery on the African, Frazier concluded that no respect was shown for the African concept of what was normal or what was expected in sexual behavior. Therefore, he contended that the Black sexual appetite, which he leaves undefined, was not extinguished during this process and consequently, in considering the sex life of the American Black, *"one must begin with the fundamental fact that at the beginning of his history in the United States, his sexual behavior was determined by raw sex impulses and that these impulses were restrained by the discipline of the plantation regime"*. The legacy of assumed inferiority and savagery of the African slave descendants as a consequence of slavery is an inheritance which crippled Frazier's full and proper understanding of Black social reality.

This paralysis came about in part as a result of Frazier accepting the removal of Africa as a central focus of the analysis of Black reality. It is of interest that Frazier supported his contention that African culture had no influence on the development of the New World Black family with the work of Robert Parks, his White mentor, who argued that due to the manner in which Africans were enslaved and dispersed in America, African tradition could not have taken root and survived in the United States. One must, of course, point out that Robert Parks' "scientific" contributions were made in the early 1900's and there is no reason to believe that he was any more immune to the legacy of Malthus than his contemporaries, Hall, Thorndike, Terman, and Ferguson. By accepting the thinking of another race, the "paralyzed" are traditionally immobilized from providing the necessary insight for understanding Black reality.

As noted earlier, the ideas of science and the interest of science, and, even the definition of science are bound in the time and historical condition of the society in which its developers live. The ideas, interest, application and definition of science go on in a human world; and, life is subjective. Science, without question, is a political weapon. The science with which we grapple today was, without question, influenced by the way in which its developers came to understand reality. Since science is a reconstruction of reality and ideology is an instrument which influences the awareness of reality, science can only reconstruct the awareness which ideology provides. Hence, when the social reality is defined by racism and oppression or in a society where the prevailing ideology is racist, there can be no science which is not, in fact, oppressive and racist. Science in the west is, in fact, a reconstruction of racism. One need only note that just as science served this society in the creation and use of technical and industrial power, it also has served in the creation and use of theories and ideas designed to control the use of power by its oppressed, especially New World Africans.

With the exception of paralyzing Black intellectual analyses, this use of science to define reality and in so doing, control the thinking of Black people, has never been completely successful. The reason for this failure is due, in fact, to the role of ideology in the meaning of science.

Ideology emerges and takes form (becomes objective) in response to a people's consciousness and condition. In referring to the work of Shils, Karenga (1978) notes that ideology develops, or more correctly a counter ideology[4] develops because there is an objective need for it. In a way, the very conditions that oppress a people create in part the necessary social consciousness which will resist that oppression. As Karenga points out, Shils noted that *"an ideology arises because there are strongly felt needs which are not satisfied by the prevailing outlook, for an explanation of important experiences ... and legitimization of the value and dignity of the persons who feel these needs"*. It is important to add to this view that ideology as a tool for explaining experiences does not develop solely as a pure reaction to the conditions being experienced. In the case of the dehumanization of a people the counter ideology will develop as a consequence of both their cultural consciousness prior to their oppression and the conditions which define that oppression. Hence, the counter ideology is a product of the current concrete conditions and the people's historical consciousness.

The question of "knowing" and the use of science as a reconstruction or reality for Black thinkers was, therefore, complicated by (1) the implicit racist ideology imbedded in the prevailing definition of science; and, (2) the simultaneous emergence of a counter ideology as a consequence in part, of our dehumanization and oppression, on the one hand and historical consciousness, on the other.

CHAPTER THREE

Scientific Inquiry :
Empirical and
Theoretical
Considerations for
Defining Black
Families

Chapter 3

Scientific Inquiry: Empirical and Theoretical Considerations For Defining Black Families

In order to establish an empirical and theoretical framework for the study of Black Family life, one has to immediately assess the question of what constitutes scientific inquiry. Professor Jones (1976) of Howard University has noted that systematic scientific inquiry begins where common sense leaves off. In fact, common sense or the sense of a people constitutes the base upon which scientific information is built. Scientific inquiry is, therefore, idiosyncratic to the people upon whose common sense it is built . The social scientist's task, in fact, is to extend the common sense wisdom of one's people by reducing that element of reality with which we are concerned to "intellectually manageable properties" without compromising its empirical truth. The social scientist's role is, therefore, to present the "truth" of one's people in a scientific manner. The purpose of science is to extend or expand the common sense understanding of one's people with scientific understanding.

In recognition that the goal of science is to

understand phenomena and not singularly to predict and control phenomena, the task of scientific inquiry is to establish general laws about the phenomena, which, in turn, serve as instruments for systematic explanation and which provide the basis for dependable prediction. The source of difficulty in the establishment of these general laws (particularly for social phenomena, i.e., Black family life) has been : 1) a limited definition of the procedure for obtaining factual information and 2) a limited capacity to understand the information obtained. In the domain of science, both these issues have limited our ability to develop an adequate theoretical and empirical framework for understanding the Black family.

In the area of social scientific inquiry it is generally believed that controlled experimentation is the best method for obtaining factual knowledge. It is, therefore, argued that advanced theoretical development cannot be achieved without systematic experimentation. Hence, the paucity of reliable laws found in each of the social science disciplines is seen as the direct result of the paucity of systematic experimentation. That is to say, the procedure for obtaining factual information is controlled experimentation; and very little controlled experimentation occurs in the social scientific disciplines. Therefore, very few general laws are determined.

It is, however, true, as Nagel (1961) points out, that in other branches of inquiry the lack of an opportunity or even desire to engage in controlled experiments has not prevented the scientist from arriving at well-grounded general laws. Nagel notes, for instance, that astronomy in terms of the stability of its comprehensive theory and accuracy of its predictions, as a science, has been judged superior to many other branches of science. It has obtained this position without "experimentally manipulating the celestial bodies". It is, in fact, true that many branches of science have contributed, and continue to do so, to the advancement of generalized knowledge despite severe limitations on their abilities to perform controlled experiments.

The advancement of general reliable knowledge, however, does require a systematic procedure: a procedure which contains the essentials of scientific inquiry, i.e., 1) care in observation, and 2) occurrences which manifest variation in factors. The "controlled investigation" procedure outlined by Nagel consists of a deliberate search for contrasting occasions (where the phenomenon is either uniformly manifested or manifested in some cases but not others) and the examination of certain factors in these occasions (in order to ascertain whether variations in these factors are related to differences in the phenomenon). This procedure meets the requirements of systematic inquiry while simultaneously eliminating the constraints of controlled experimentation on the social phenomenon.

The expansion of the procedures associated with achieving reliable information will not in itself, however, result in general laws regarding, in this case, Black family life; nor will it release us from the legacy of utilizing non-Black interpretive or analytical frameworks. In order for this to be accomplished, one has to combine the procedural expansion (i.e., controlled investigation) with a culturally sensitive capacity for understanding the information obtained via the systematic controlled investigation.

This second consideration raises the issue of the "differential capacity to understand" as a problem for scientific inquiry. For instance, given that one engages in a controlled investigation of Black family lifestyles and searches for contrasting occasions where aspects of Black family life are either uniformly manifested or present in some cases but not others, and examines factors in those occasions in order to ascertain whether variations in these factors are related to differences in Black family lifestyles, one's ability to establish general laws is still limited by the capacity to understand the information derived from this procedure.

Merton (1973) has argued that the "capacity to understand" is central to the "insider/outsider" doctrine. In its strongest form, the insider/outsider doctrine puts forth the claim as a matter of epistemological principle that particular groups have a monopolistic access to certain kinds of knowledge and therefore, have a greater capacity to understand. The argument would hold, therefore, that as a matter of social epistemology, only Black historians have the capacity to understand Black history or only Black sociologists would have the capacity to understand the social life of Black people. In short, Merton argues that because the outsiders, by definition, have not been socialized in the target group's culture, nor have they been engaged in the panorama of experiences associated with the life of that group, they do not have the direct, intuitive sensibility necessary for (empathetic) understanding. Merton goes on to point out, with some skepticism, that only through continued socialization in the life of a group can one become "fully aware of its symbolisms, definition of socially shared realities, and meanings of behavior, feelings and values" which are critical to understanding the unwritten grammar of conduct and nuances of their cultural idiom. Consequently, the insider/outsider doctrine argues that the outsider has a structurally imposed incapacity to comprehend alien groups, cultures, societies, etc. The result of this structural incapacity is that the insider and the outsider must arrive at different (and presumably incompatible) findings and interpretations even when they examine the same phenomena. The insider/outsider doctrine would, therefore, predict that Black and White researchers on the Black family would arrive at different interpretations and conclusions about the Black family. This, however, has not been the case. He goes on, in fact, to discuss the impact of "structural differentiation" and "social status sets".

In terms of structural differentiation and status sets, Merton questions the position of the insider's privileged capacity to understand by noting that human beings in socially differentiated societies can, in fact, be located in a single social status category or in several categories. The crucial fact of social structure is that individuals do not have a single status but a complement of variously inter-related statuses, or what is called a "status set". The array of status sets in a population means that aggregates of individuals share some statuses and not others. In effect, individuals are both insiders and outsiders. Accordingly, Merton concludes that the idiomatic expression of the total insider doctrine; i.e., one must be one in order to understand one, is "deceptively simple and sociologically fallacious". However, before dismissing the argument that one's possession of a status set reduces the claim of special capacity to understand as the consequence of belonging to a particular status, one has to point out that the inadequacy of the total insider argument as treated by Merton, is probably true in the sociological domain. However, the "truths" of psychology suggest that given the diversity of sociological status or even multiple status sets, the differential power attributed to a single status can render it as the filter through which all other perspectives associated with other statuses are screened. For instance, the psychological meaning or power associated with the ascribed status, race (in a racist society), would in all probability be stronger or more influential in terms of perceiving reality than the achieved status of middle-class. Accordingly, one's perceptions about reality stemming from one's status as middle-class would be filtered through the more psychologically powerful screen (status) of Blackness. The psychological power given to a particular status can be such that it can influence the "relevance" of all other statuses and become the dominant criterion for defining reality. Hence, psychologically, "being one is necessary if you are to fully understand one", or less idiomatically, having been socialized [5] in the psycho-cultural medium of a group, one is more aware of that group's symbolisms, definitions of socially shared reality and their meanings of behavior, feelings and values. Hence, I would argue that the "capacity to understand" is related to one's status as an insider (i.e., a psychocultural insider). I would not, however, argue that one's status as an insider guarantees an understanding of the phenomena. In fact, because of the racial and cultural oppression of Black people, Black people, especially in the academic arena, are forced to examine the world through glasses ground fine in order to focus reality for White people. The analogy of course, suggests that our vision is distorted because of the glasses we wear and not because our eyesight (insider status) is poor.

This suggests a plausible explanation for why Black social scientists have not determined an analysis and discussion of the Black family significantly different from that of White researchers. Even though Black social scientists have a special sensitivity to the psycho-cultural reality of Black life, the formal process of examining that reality scientifically has placed real perceptual and, therefore interpretive, constraints on our analysis. Scientifically, we have, too often, "seen through eyes whitely".

In his discussion of the scientific method, Mark Jones (1976) identified, and noted as did Nagel (1969) before him, that scientific

inquiry begins where common sense leaves off
and that the fundamental purpose of that
inquiry is to "allow people to anticipate future
events and to develop strategies to maximize
our control over them".   Jones argues that
every researchable problem occurs within a
network defined by a people's anticipation and
control of needs.

The three critical points in this network or
web of anticipation and control of needs are
the people's : 1) world-view, 2) set of
normative assumptions; and 3) frame of
reference.   In addition to answering specific
questions like, who are we?, where did we
come from?, how did we get here?, and where
do we wish to go?, a people's world-view also
defines what they believe to be their "nature"
and the way in which the world should
operate.   Growing directly out of their world-
view, the normative assumptions of a people
summarize their perception of the nature of
the "good life" and the political, economic,
and cultural forms and/or processes necessary
for the realization of that life.   Jones rightfully
notes that academic disciplines develop
directly within the context of these two
features.

A people's frame of reference, which is
more directly related to academic disciplines
and scientific inquiry, serves as the "lens"
through which a people perceives the
experiential world.   It particularly structures
the rules of concept formation and determines
the major concepts, propositions and theories
appropriate to the examination of reality.   In
effect, it prescribes the assumptions and issues
which will be considered as "legitimate" areas

of study. These three concepts (world-view, normative assumptions and frame of reference) are defining factors in what we will discuss below as "conceptual incarceration" and "transubstantiation"; and, as such are the keys to : 1) unlocking or freeing ourselves from the legacy of White scholarship, and 2) defining a Black theoretical analysis of the Black family.

CHAPTER FOUR

Transubstantiation
and Conceptual
Incarceration:
Epistemological
Problems in the
Analysis of Black
Reality

Chapter 4

Transubstantiation and Conceptual Incarceration: Epistemological Problems in the Analysis of Black Reality

When we consider the process by which symbolism, meanings, definitions, feelings, attitudes, values, and behavior are transmitted to each and every member of a group, one is immediately compelled to deal with a notion of culture. In global terms, culture is the composite montage of specific ways of thinking, feeling and acting, which is peculiar to the members of a particular group and which, in its combined form, distinguishes that group from other groups. That is to say, the dominant tone or unique rhythm of a particular montage distinguishes it from other cultural montages. To follow that analogy out, it does not suggest that one culture has a monopoly on color or pattern of notes. It simply states that the particular blend of colors or pattern of notes defining one culture distinguishes it from other cultures. Accordingly, it is the blends and tones in their combined form which give a particular image (perspective) to a culture. Hence, in response to the Mertonian argument, one must recognize that it is the cultural montage wholistically and not the elemental differentiation of one's multiple status sets which influences one's perception of reality. It is, accordingly, membership in a particular cultural montage which gives one a greater "capacity to understand" information relevant to that cultural group. Specific to a people's cultural montage is a particular "belief system". Parenthetically, it is the people's belief system which speaks to or reflects their worldview, normative assumptions and frame of reference.

Hence, it is through an accurate understanding of a particular group's belief system that the social scientist is able to accurately interpret the "outcomes" of that particular group's human processes.

Transubstantiation (cf: Von Lue, 1975) is a process wherein the cultural substance of one culture is transformed into the cultural substance of another culture. Every act of cognition implies some form of transubstantiation. In terms of different cultures, the process amounts to a kind of "elemental" translation or substance transformation. To follow the analogy made above, transubstantiation would be a process wherein the defining rhythm of one culture is translated into the rhythm of another culture.

When the cultural orientation, or more understandably, the "belief system" of one culture as seen and defined by the people of that culture is translated or transformed into the cultural orientation or belief system of another culture as seen and defined by the people of the second culture then an act of transubstantiation has occurred. To the extent that a people's "understanding" of their world as interpreted in their meanings, definitions, feelings, values, etc., is lost and/or distorted in the translation of the "understanding" via the meanings, definitions, feelings, etc. belonging to another people, one has a "transubstantive error".   When   the   social   scientist   or researcher doesn't respect the integrity of a people's "cultural perspective", he is prone to fall   victim   to   the   above-   mentioned "transubstantive error", an error wherein one defines or interprets the behavior and/or medium of one culture with "meanings" appropriate to and consistent with another culture. To the extent that the people of, for example, Culture X's understanding of their world is lost or distorted when interpreted with or through the belief system of the people of Culture Y, one has a transubstantive error. When, for instance, the European encountered the African, the translation of the African experience   (as   seen   and   defined   and understood by the African) by the European was an act of transubstantiation. Because of the fact that the African world-view, normative assumptions, and frame of reference were all different from the European worldview, normative   assumptions,   and   frame   of reference, it is not surprising that most, if not all, of the African experience would be misinterpreted and misunderstood.   An analysis of the "scientific" treatment of the African peoples by non-African scholars will reveal   more   than   just   an   occasional transubstantive error.

For   example,   the   cultural   substance associated with the African milieu was such that Africans believed the universe to be a "vitalistic pneumaticism" (Thomas, 1960). That is, the African believed the universe to be alive. Consequently, the African's relation to the universe was characterized by a belief in the paramount and primary importance of life. Because Africans believed all things in the universe to be endowed with the same Supreme Force or life spirit (the breath of God), they also believed that all things were the same on one level while different, yet interconnected and interdependent on another level. The primary supreme integrity of life, or the life force, can be considered as consistent with an African cultural substance.

When one examines the African reality with African normative assumptions and a frame of reference based on or reflective of an African world-view, one is immediately struck with the emphasis on life and fertility expressed or manifested in African culture. African art, for instance, has a high concentration of life as evidenced by statues of fertility gods and goddesses, pregnant women, and men with erections. When these cultural elements or artifacts, as seen and defined by Africans, were transformed into European elements, as seen and defined by Europeans, the "life force" as consistent with the African orientation was given a "sexual" meaning. The African focus on fertility and life was seen as meaning sexual or emphasizing sex with strong Oedipal implications. Here we can see the "transubstantive error". An analysis of European religion and philosophy would reveal a particular concern and emphasis on sexuality. Similarly, an analysis of European sexuality with European psychology would suggest that sex, in this case, the denigration of sex, is a core feature of the European cultural substance. Accordingly, it was predictable that life force and its cultural manifestations (i.e. fertility) would have been misunderstood by the non-African examiners. As another example, we can note that in emphasizing the primacy of life, the African frame of reference, in turn, emphasized a particular resolute position of the woman. The woman's special importance was in her natural role of ensuring the continuity of life. The woman demonstrated and symbolized the source of life; hence, Africans, regardless of descent systems, focused on and gave special recognition to the woman. This process or what we have called the "matrifocal focus" was an African cultural perspective which, when viewed by non-Africans, became a process of "female dominance", or matriarchal family organizations. Here, again we can see an example of the cultural orientation as seen and defined by one culture being distorted when an alien culture attempts to define that cultural orientation in alien terms and through an alien framework.

Because the normative assumptions of a people prescribe their "method" for obtaining that which is defined as "good" by them, it too becomes an area of possible error. In African culture, for instance, the "method" for obtaining that which is good is found in the African's ability to "manipulate" the powers or forces of the universe. Accordingly, individuals do not compete with each other. One person's understanding of the "powers", and their ability to manipulate these powers may be greater than another's; hence, one person can achieve more than another not because of individual competitiveness, but rather because of greater understanding or skill. Predictably, the transubstantive error would occur when one simply "sees" competition in the African cultural setting and defines that on the basis of individual rivalry, which is a European normative assumption. The transubstantive error would also be true if Africans, seeing "competition" in the European setting, defined it in terms of "manipulations of power".

The importance of transubstantiation and subsequent transubstantive errors is compounded in instances like the above. This is particularly true in two different cultures where there is evidence of the same external or overt behavioral expression, cultural artifact, or status set . One can only be sure of what one knows, when one eliminates or reduces the transubstantive error. The potential for committing the transubstantive error is decreased as one increases the understanding of the cultural substance of a particular people as seen and defined by that particular group of people.

The failure of Black social scientists to recognize and respect our own cultural substance has not only forced us to commit the same "transubstantive errors" as our White counterparts, it has also led to a condition wherein our thinking has been incarcerated in an intellectual prism defined by the cultural substance of White reality. It seems evident that an accurate representation of Black reality is dependent upon the Black social scientist's ability to assist in the reconceptualization and reconstruction of Black reality independently of White conceptualizations [6].

It has become more and more evident that, while we have been thoroughly trained in a body of scientific inquiry purporting to examine the complexities of the human condition, upon closer examination, our formal training only provides limited understanding of the psycho-cultural reality of White people. Consequently, we have been incarcerated in conceptual assumptions associated with Euro-American analytical frameworks. This we have defined as conceptual incarceration.

In brief, we have been trained to accept as the only world-view, the normative assumptions and frame of reference, the prism of White perspectives (i.e., White world-view, normative assumptions, and frame of reference). Consequently, we have been entrapped in an epistemological dilemma. The dominant feature of this dilemma has been to assume that the "behavior" of Black people and White people should be the same. This would be similar to assuming that the behavior of the prisoner and the guard are the same, or, even worse, that the "behavior of the prisoner", and the prisoner, are one and the same. The insidious aspect of the epistemological trap is the process wherein the Black social scientists accept a set of White defined assumptions about Black people and proceed to utilize those assumptions in the study of our people. Predictably, this legacy has resulted in Black scholars being forced to rationalize the negativity of their own so-called results. The state of conceptual incarceration inhibits us from asking the right questions. Hence, we are limited in what we can know about Black social reality by what we think we know about the dynamics of social reality in general (which more accurately should be called, White social reality). The meta-epistemological dilemma for Black social scientists is that we find ourselves seeking an awareness of our own reality, yet the parameters of the definition of what constitutes knowledge about reality is defined according to the (White) conceptions of reality. To work without recognizing and resolving this dilemma is to be conceptually incarcerated.

It is through an accurate understanding of a particular group's belief system that the social scientist is able to accurately interpret the "outcomes" of that particular group's human processes. It is the people's belief system which reveals their cultural montage, and in so doing, reflects their world-view, normative assumptions and frame of reference, in effect, their ideological premise. Without understanding the belief system of a people, one cannot interpret their ideological premise. Serious errors have been made concerning the nature of Black life as a consequence of the misinterpretation and delegitimation of our culture. These errors, though clearly the results of ideological racism, we have defined as transubstantive in nature.

The potential for committing the transubstantive error is decreased as one increases the understanding of the cultural substance of a particular people as seen and defined by that particular group of people.

In cross-cultural research, one can only be

sure of what one knows when one eliminates or reduces the transubstantive error. To work without recognizing and resolving this dilemma is to be conceptually incarcerated.

In order, therefore, to free ourselves from the legacy and to begin the process of defining a Black theoretical analysis of the Black family, we must understand the African and African-American cultural substance and build an analysis from that cultural perspective, normative assumptions, and frame of reference.

CHAPTER FIVE

Back to the Roots :
African Culture As
A Basis For
Understanding
Black Families

Chapter 5

Back To The Roots: African Culture As A Basis For Understanding Black Families

In a sense, the cultural world-view characterizing a particular group of people functions like a special set of glasses which, in focusing on reality, perceives and is aware of those situations which are meaningful and excludes those which are not.   Hence, it is primarily through this special set of glasses that the myriad of sensory impressions received by the organism are filtered, organized, and transformed into mental impressions and behavioral dispositions and/or responses. This means also, of course, that culture or the cultural world-view functions like a set of "blinders" which obscures, misperceives, or completely fails to perceive at all, aspects of the total reality.   In a way, culture is likened to a programmer in computer operations. It has a code or set of instructions which organizes the reception of "sensory" data, rejects inappropriate information, accepts the appropriate, refers it to the store of past associations, ideas, and knowledge, processes it and defines a solution, or in this case, defines an interpretation of the meaning of "reality".

Although there probably is no commonly accepted "standard" definition of culture, the most important criterion or feature is that culture is a set or sets of shared behavior and ideas which are symbolic, systematic, cumulative, and transmitted from generation to generation . It is the montage of a people. A people's culture is the vast structure of language, customs, knowledge, ideas, and values which provide a people with a general design for living and patterns for interpreting reality.   As part of the people's world-view, cultural values particularly help to define, select, create and re-create (or reformulate) what is considered good, valuable or desirable in the social milieu.

It is our contention that Black culture in the United States is the result of a special mixture of our continued African orientation operating within another cultural milieu which is primarily defined by the philosophical assumptions and underpinnings of the Anglo-American community.   Accordingly, it is that African perspective which is at the base of the Black cultural sphere.   Similarly, it is the continuation of that African worldview which is at the root of the special features in Black life styles.   It is the continuation of the African orientation which, in part, helps to define the "general design for living and the patterns for interpreting reality" for, or characteristic of, Black people.

In order to demonstrate this contention, a brief discussion of traditional African belief systems, particularly as it relates to family, is necessary.

Traditional African Belief System: In relation to
the family, it is important to understand the
particular philosophical, ontological, and
cosmological understanding of the universe
belonging to the people under examination. In
terms of the notion of family, the implicit
African cosmological (Oneness of Being) and
ontological (Nature of Being is Force, Spirit)
understanding, along with the particular
definitions of "time" and "space" within these
cosmological and ontological dimensions,
suggest that the family constitutes the center
of one's being or existence.

Cosmologically, individual consciousness
was such that the family constituted the
reference point wherein one's existence was
perceived as being interconnected to the
existence of all else. On this point, Mbiti
(1970) observed that, for Africans, the
individual owed his very existence to all the
members (living, dead and yet-to-be-born) of
the family, tribe, or clan. Mbiti further notes
that the individual did not and could not exist
alone. The individual was an integral part of
the collective unity, i.e., the family. In
recognition of this kind of awareness, others
(Mbiti, 1970, Nobles, 1976b) have noted that
the traditional African view of "self" is
contingent upon the actual existence of others.

Ontologically [7], the African belief system
understood that the nature of all things in the
universe was "force" or "spirit" (cf: Tempels,
1959). It is logical, or at least consistent,
therefore, that in believing that all things,
including man, were endowed with the same
Supreme Force, one would also believe that all
things are "essentially" one. For the African,

the world-view is based on the ontological identification of "being (existence) in the universe" as being characterized by a cosmological "participation in the Supreme Force". Parenthetically, it is understandable that if ontologically the African believes that the nature of all things is force, the African would, accordingly, view the variety of cosmic beings as quantitative alterations of the same Supreme Force (cf: Thomas, 1961). That is, the classification of "beings" and the "level of being" becomes a classification of forces or spirits.

For the African, a natural feature of the universe is the multiplicity of forms and moments. What characterizes African peoples' understanding of the universe is, consequently, a simultaneous respect for the concrete detail in the multiplicity of forms and the rejection of the possibility of an absence or vacuum of forms.

The African conception of the world and phenomena within it amounts to a set of synthesis (connections) and contradictions (antagonisms) linked to the particular classification of beings as differential quantifications of force. Combined, these "connective" and "antagonistic" participatory sets form the whole of universal relations. Accordingly, Africans traditionally believed that relations in the universe are determined by elements belonging to the same metaphysical plane, "participating by difference" (cf: Thomas, 1961). The dynamic quality of the total universe is, however, thought to be the conciliation of these various "participatory sets". In fact, the conciliation of, on the one hand, the unity of the cosmos and, on the other, the diverseness of beings within the cosmos, makes for the special features (e.g., dynamism, interdependence, variety, optimism, etc.) of the traditional world-view.

In recognition that the quality of the universe is vitalistic, the notions of time and space within the "universal picture" are affected by that life force. Time, for instance, is conceived as a plurality. It is both ontological and empirical. Ontological time is the awareness of the vital force. It is being aware of the "drama of life", the nature of events and the existence of beings. In effect, ontological time is a "dramatic conscience" (cf: Thomas, 1961). In the Western sense of quantification, time or the awareness of ontological time, cannot be measured. As noted, the plurality of African times does include a comprehension of time which is empirical. "Empirical time" is comprised of two essential aspects. Here, time is descriptively vitalistic, in that it is at the same time rhythmic (changing) and stable (permanent). In accordance with the cosmological and ontological features of the African conception of the universe, the "permanent" aspect of empirical time perceives time as the "essence of God", i.e., the stable element (constant feature) in the universal structure. Rhythmically, empirical time is also seen as reflecting the natural process of change, i.e., the dynamic element (variable feature) in the universal structure. Mythically, this rhythmic aspect is oftentimes referred to as the "heartbeat of God".

The universe, spatially, like its temporal
feature, is also seen as vitalistic. That is, the
spatial character of the universe is "vibrative".
The spatial dimensions of the universe are
seen as "vibrating" to the rhythmic quality of a
natural harmony.   Space, in the African
conception, is "elastic" as opposed to
"concrete".   The vibrations of this space
rhythmically expand and diminish to the
extent that the spatial elements in the cosmos
match the pulsations of the ontological rhythm
of the universe.   The cosmological and
ontological connection of "time" and "space"
are, understandably, such that the universe is
understood as, conceived as, and believed to
be, a living "vitalistic pneumaticism" .

As noted earlier, the notion of self, in
accordance with the African belief system, was
based on one's individual consciousness taking
as its reference point, the family, wherein
one's existence is perceived as   being
interconnected to the existence of all else.
More specifically, we can note that the
traditional philosophical notion of Oneness of
Being requires that man conceptualizes his
own existence as being an awareness of his
universal connectedness, i.e., man is an
indispensable, integrated, and interdependent
part of the universe.   The notions of
Interdependence and Oneness of Being allow
for a conception of self which transcends,
throughout the historical consciousness of
one's people, the finiteness of both the
physical body, finite space and absolute time.
The notion of self, or more specifically, the
awareness of self for African peoples, is,
therefore, not limited to just the cognitive

awareness of one's own uniqueness, individuality and historical finiteness. In its truest form, it is self-awareness which is the awareness of one's historical consciousness (collective spirituality and the subsequent state or sense of "we-ness"). The most compelling property of the traditional notion of self is the process of cosmologically grounding the self in the collective, social and spiritual sense of the history of one's people. In recognition of this kind of self-awareness, which is consistent with a particular belief system, we can note that the traditional African (and most contemporary descendants) view of "self" is contingent upon the existence of other.

The dynamic quality of the total universe is thought to be the conciliation of various "participatory sets" (i.e., connective and antagonistic). Similarly, it is this philosophical conciliation which allows us to recognize simultaneously that (1) African families do vary from time 1 to time 2, from one locale to another and even from one family to another, and (2) that no matter what form (variety, type, or style) they take, the notion of family or clan is considered, regardless of the time and space parameters of one's presence, to be the most important entity. The clan across African family systems is believed to be a sort of total entity, of which its members - like the elemental structure of the universe - are integral and interconnected parts.

Existence is therefore at the level of the family. That is, family existence is more important than individual existence. As an aside, we can note that in terms of the notion of "genetic proximity", wherein simplistically, the "begetter is always more 'powerful' than the offspring", the family entity constitutes more power or force than the individual entity. Accordingly, family existence is "paramount" to individual existence and, to paraphrase Jean-Paul Sartre, the family essence precedes the individual existence.

The family, which includes the living, the dead, and those yet-to-be-born (Erny, 1973) was thought to be, therefore, the center or focal point, wherein the essence of the community (of peoplehood) is kept alive. The family is based on the unity and diversity of people and processes. The family is the center of existence. It is the center of the universe.

It is evident that the traditional African belief system was passed down from generation to generation as discussed above. The African belief system was transmitted from generation to generation by the same mechanism or process which influences the actual awareness of reality, i.e., human socialization. Socialization is the process by which we cause ourselves to internalize and reflect a particular world-view, normative assumptions and frame of reference. Like culture itself, the socialization process [8] influences our perception of, knowledge about, and understanding of, social reality.

Having been victims of physical and psychological enslavement, and having been educated away from our traditional world-view and belief system, a true understanding of Black social reality, particularly Black family life, will only become a reality when Black social scientists become re-sensitized to our own culture and use it as the interpretive framework for our social scientific analyses. Without question, the failure of Black research and scholarship, particularly Black family research, has been the inability of researchers and scholars to re-think the issue and to conceive of the Black experience in terms of its own integrity.

Role of Culture: More so than the Black social scientist, the Black artist, particularly Paul Robeson, has seen the connection between culture and the oppression of Black people. Paul Robeson, as the Black artist, throughout most of his career, saw culture as an instrument in a people's liberation and conversely, the suppression or denial of culture as an instrument of their enslavement.

Amilcar Cabral(1973) noted more formally in this regard that oppression or domination of a people is only secured when the cultural life of a people is destroyed, paralyzed, or at least neutralized.Parenthetically, it may in fact be the case that the different forms of oppression experienced by African people are determined by the emphasis placed on destroying, paralyzing or neutralizing the culture of the people under domination

Cabral goes on to note that the ideal situation for foreign domination is either to liquidate practically all the dominated people or to harmonize the oppressor's economic and political (ideological) domination of the people without damaging the culture of the dominated. The "dilemma of culture" is one wherein culture naturally resists its own oppression and the act of oppression requires the elimination of that which naturally resists it. Cabral correctly recognized that in order to

escape this "dilemma of culture", the
oppressor has to create "scientific" theories
which secure the domination of the people and
their resources. The use of science or the
continual creation of theories have, in fact,
been translated into a permanent state of siege
of African peoples. In many respects, science,
or more correctly, western science,
particularly social science, like the economic
and political institutions, has become an
instrument designed to reflect the culture of
the oppressor and to allow for the more
efficient domination and oppression of African
people.

As noted above, the failure of Black social
scientists to recognize and respect our own
cultural substance has not only caused us to
commit the same "transubstantive errors" as
our White counterparts, it has also led to a
condition wherein Black social scientific
thinking has been defined by the cultural
substance (ideology) of White reality. It is this
latter condition which has forced Black social
scientists to become unwilling participants in
the scientific oppression of our own people. It
seems evident that, in the future, an accurate
representation of Black reality and the
subsequent enhancement of Black life will be
dependent upon the Black social scientist's
realization that science in its true meaning is,
in part, a reconstruction of a people's
ideological premise. It is, however, extremely
important to recognize that one can create a
reconstruction which is not a reflection or
explanation of a people's reality, but an
"idealization" of it . That is, in reconstructing
the common sense of a people's wisdom, the

resultant science can represent what reality would be if it were extracted and refined to purity or what it should be if one controlled (eliminated or dismissed) the effects of real conditions. Clearly, one can see that "idealizations" can be carried so far that they are useful only for the further development of "reconstructions" or they are internalized by the people and become part of their common sense set. In both cases, such activity does not provide an accurate understanding or evaluation of the people's reality. In the first case, the reconstruction may become so idealized or abstract that upon its application, one loses sight of the phenomenon or reality initially under examination. In the second case, the idealization becomes confused with the common sense wisdom, and to the extent that the reconstruction was inconsistent with the common sense, the people become culturally transformed. It is in this latter example that science has become an insidious political institution which assists in the oppression and domination of African peoples.

When Black scholars accept the same assumptions and frameworks as White researchers, we end up with the same conclusions, or we make the same type of errors. For instance, the main theme of Frazier's classic work on the Black family (cf: Frazier, 1932) contended, in fact, that the distortion and pathology found in Black families was mainly the product of slavery and racism. Frazier's scientific training, however, was based on the world-view and normative assumptions of White Americans. Consequently, his implicit frame of reference,

like those of his mentors, was that White
people and their way of life was the standard
against which all else should be measured.
Accordingly, it was the general belief that
American culture was, by definition,
synonymous with the White American culture.

Frazier assumed a common cultural reality
between Blacks and Whites which, in turn,
allowed him to adopt a common framework for
interpreting their respective family lifestyles.
Such an assumption places Frazier's landmark
research in the category of conceptually
incarcerated research with its associated
transubstantive errors. The cultural
homogeneity approach, as reflected by the
work of Frazier, as well as many others,
assumed that American culture solely
influenced or determined Black family life. It
is, therefore, clear that, having accepted that
assumption, these scholars had to attempt to
define the elements or features of Black
families in terms of the "meaning" of elements
or features defined by American (White) family
life.

Frazier's classic study of the Black middle-
class committed the transubstantive error, in
terms of consumptive patterns. Frazier
described, for example, the lack of regard for
the protestant ethic (as seen and defined by
middle-class White Anglo-Saxon protestant
culture) which emphasized the accumulation of
wealth as an index of the Black bourgeoisie's
failure to internalize "genuine" middle-class
values. This he concludes in terms of
observable outcomes, i.e., Black consumptive
activities. What he didn't do, primarily
because of the a priori assumption of cultural

homogeneity, was to see and define
"consumptive activities" as a cultural element
definable in terms of Black cultural reality. It
was (is) not true that Black consumptive
activities were (are) an indicator of Black
families "failing" to be like White families. To
the contrary, they may be an expression of a
trait that is related to the continuation of a
cultural orientation specific to people of
African descent.

African peoples, traditionally, are not a
money-oriented people, in the sense of
hoarding money for the sake of having capital.
Money itself is not important. The value, in
fact, of money is in its provision of goods and
services. Money, therefore, is not generally
saved for saving sake. It is consumed. Hence,
the transubstantive error for Frazier was in
defining consumptive activities as an example
of Black "failure", which nicely fits into the
mosaic of social pathology and disorganization.

A more systematic analysis of the work of
Liebow, (1969), Rainwater (1970), Moynihan
(!965) and Bernard (1966), and the host of
other social scientific bedfellows, would
probably reveal more than just an occasional
"transubstantive error". Clearly, to reject the
cultural integrity of Black people leads to a
transubstantive error.

The potential for committing the
transubstantive error, however, is decreased as
one increases his understanding of the
"cultural substance" of a particular people, as
seen and defined by that particular group of
people. Accordingly, one of the tasks of Black
social scientists is to become conscious of our
own consciousness (which is very different

from being aware of "accepted" perceptions of reality). It is our task to develop our intrinsic African apperception and then develop and practice a discipline and scientific inquiry which is (pre-) determined by the particular way in which we understand and are conscious of our own awareness of reality.

In implying that Black social scientific investigations must be rooted in the nature of the Black culture, which in turn is rooted in, or based on, an African world-view, it is further implied consequently, that the dominant aspect of Black social scientific inquiry must reflect an African-American world-view, normative assumptions and frame of reference. Black social scientific inquiry must be consistent with our language, customs, knowledge, ideas, values, beliefs, and symbolisms.

Clearly, the "conceptual incarceration" of Black family research in the legacy of White defined analytical frameworks will only end when Black scholars begin to conceive of the Black family independently of conceptualizations of White families. That is to say, a full and accurate understanding of the Black family will only occur when it is conceptualized, studied, and evaluated in terms of its own intrinsic definition. A task such as this requires, in itself, new theory, new analytical frameworks, and new research models.

CHAPTER SIX

Africanity : A
Theoretical and
Empirical
Framework

Chapter 6

Africanity: A Theoretical and Empirical Framework

Without question, the fundamental proposition historically affecting Black people in the New World has been cultural domination. The twin instruments of this domination have, of course, been "racism" and "economic exploitation". Parenthetically, it should be emphasized that racism and exploitation are at the source of any ontological changes in Black people. However, because the examination of Black reality has been done with non-Black analytical instruments, the real changes in Black people have not been revealed or recorded. The world-view of the scientists does influence their inquiry. Several studies have suggested, in fact, that the general "world-view" of psychologists, for instance, influences both the questions they ask and the methods they adopt to find and interpret the answers. It is also suggested that the world-view influence is probably greater than the influence stemming from relations with other psychologists.[9]

The direct consequence of a particular cultural orientation influencing social scientific inquiry has been the distortion of any social reality which, in its psycho-cultural fabric, didn't match or wasn't consistent or appropriate to that orientation. The real consequence of investigation of Black people being incarcerated in the world-view of White Americans has been that our scientific understanding of Black social reality, particularly Black family life, has been for the most part determined by the indices and frame of reference (i.e., racism, White supremacy and exploitation) of the world-view of the traditional White social scientist.

As stated above, it is our contention that Black culture in the United States is the result of a special admixture of our continued African world-view operating within another cultural milieu which is primarily defined by the philosophical assumptions and underpinnings of the Anglo-American community. Accordingly, it is that African world-view which is at the base of the Black cultural sphere. Similarly, it is the continuation of that African world-view which is at the root of the special features in Black lifestyles.

It is suggested, therefore, that what determines the special form Black families take and the unique relation patterns expressed by Black family systems is primarily the sense of "Africanity". Parenthetically, it should be noted that the sense of "Africanity" in Black families does not require the pre-supposition of a homogeneous, monolithic Black family type, nor does it mean that Black families are culturally stagnant or dormant. There is diversity in Black families; however, within that diversity one is able to discern a comprehensive cultural theme which has historically characterized Black families. It is this cultural screen (theme) or commonality which we refer to as the sense of "Africanity".

Axiomatically, therefore, we have accepted the fact that Black families are African-based families. Consequently, the study of research on Black family life must take as its theoretical model and/or conceptual framework the African philosophical world-view as reflected in contemporary Black family life. Hence, the Black family (or what is meant by the term which classified a particular set of biological, spiritual, physical and behavioral patterns and/or dynamics as a distinguishable entity) is defined by the traditional and contemporary African world-view. It is assumed, therefore it should be clear, that not only are the structural and functional features of the family dynamics a microcosmic reflection of the African conception of the universal relations, the concept of family itself is also a reflection of that conception.

In terms of the phenomena known as family systems, or more particularly, the Black family system, the logic of discovery must, therefore, proceed in first explicating the philosophical or cultural world-view which guides and defines the phenomena. This philosophy or cultural world-view is the basis for or the foundation of the family's nature or integrity. Secondly, one must develop a theoretical model and/or conceptualization which is consistent with the intrinsic philosophical world-view, and, thirdly, demonstrate the particular way in which that intrinsic world-view manifests itself and/or is affected by contemporary factors (i.e., racism, economics, etc.).

Guided by this logic, an empirical and theoretical framework for the study of Black family life must (1) explicate the philosophical positions (i.e., world-view, normative assumptions, and frame of reference) which determine the intrinsic nature or integrity of Black family systems; (2) the empirical and theoretical framework should reveal the particular way in which that world-view helps to answer questions like, who are we?, where did we come from?, how did we get here?, how should we behave?, and where do we wish to go? In terms of the last two questions, the empirical and theoretical framework must serve as an instrument through which our people can "accurately" (from our perspective) perceive the experiential world. It should, in fact, provide us with the concepts, propositions, theories, and perspectives appropriate to the examination of our reality.

As noted above, our contention is that Black culture in the United States is the result of a special admixture of our continued African world-view operating within the cultural milieu of Euro- (White) American culture. Accordingly, the world-view, normative assumptions, and frame of reference must be African-based.

A theoretical and empirical framework for defining Black social reality must, therefore, be based on African cultural residuals as reflected in the world-view, normative assumptions and frame of reference of Black people.

In ultimately recognizing this connection between science and ideology, it becomes obvious that an integral aspect of Black psychology must be the reconstruction of a Black ideology, an ideology which, I believe, finds its meaning in our definition as an African people.

Remembering that at the core of what we call "science" is a particular world-view, set of normative assumptions and referential frame, it is also important to note that these things combine to form a scientific paradigm, which guides the assessment and evaluation of reality. A paradigm is, therefore, a perceptual, cognitive and affective achievement representing the organizational process for understanding. The paradigm becomes the singular screen through which all understanding is filtered.

It, therefore, becomes obvious that the connection between science and ideology for Black thinkers must result in an African paradigm or organizational process for understanding. In order for this to come about, one of the tasks of Black psychologists should be to develop an understanding of our intrinsic African apperceptions and then to make scientific inquiries and create a social science discipline which is (pre-) determined by the particular way in which Blacks understand and are conscious of Black reality.

Accordingly, the analytical framework developed to "understand" the phenomena within a culture must be "sensitive" to the dictates of that culture. Consistent with the axiomatic contention of a continued African world-view operating within the cultural milieu of White American culture, we suggest that the Black family system should be thought of as African in "nature" and American in "nurture" (i.e., Nobles, 1974a). The intrinsic nature or integrity of Black family systems is therefore, African.

Accordingly, any proposed theoretical and empirical framework for defining Black families as well as programs for the enhancement of Black family life, must recognize that an African cultural spectrum or attitude forms the foundation of the Black cultural sphere and the wider (White) mainstream American culture serves as the medium in which the Black cultural sphere must operate. Such a framework allows us to recognize that it is the combined "continuation" of an intrinsic African (Black) value system and its reaction to the cultural imperatives of the wider American cultural milieu which determines the special features observable in Black family life.

It is extremely important to recognize that the underlying principle and basic structure/functions of the Black family is ultimately traceable to its African value system and/or some modification thereof. In order, therefore, to accurately "reflect" the dynamics of Black family life, the analysis must understand the continued intrinsic cultural spectrum of Black life in American society. For us, the best conceptualization of that continued cultural spectrum is the notion of Africanity. That is, in terms of culture and value systems (a people's common sense), the Black family should be thought of as an "Americanized African Family." It is African in nature and

American in nurture. It is both African and not African in form, structure and function. The observable behavioral outcomes of its processes must therefore be interpreted in terms of understanding (1) the African nature of basis for the outcome and (2) the American conditions which influence their development and/or expression. This in itself necessitates the need for an African reconstruction, ergo the Africanity model.

Accordingly, the research thrust to which we are associated has begun the process of defining the special features found in African-American (Black) families. Thus far, four (4) critical positions in conjunction with several special characteristics have been isolated:

Position #1: The traditional Black family is a unique cultural form enjoying its own inherent resources and/or features.

Position #2: The family itself performs important social and psychological functions.

Position #3: Some of its features may be situational (i.e., caused by the pressures of the moment) or adaptational.

Position #4: In periods of "crisis" or at "ceremonial" times, the "African nature" of the family is most visible.

Special Characteristic#1: It is comprised of several individual households, with the family definition and lines of authority and support transcending or going beyond any one household unit which comprises the "family."

Special Characteristic#2: Structurally, it expands and diminishes in response to external conditions (elasticity).

Special Characteristic #3: Child-centered system; the general purpose of family, its organization raison d'etre, focused on, if not requires the presence of children.

Special Characteristic #4: Family networking as revealed by close network of relationships between families not necessarily related by blood.

Special Characteristic #5: Role definition and performance are flexible and interchangeable. In child-rearing, a clear distinction between role definition (sex-linked) and role performance (sexless).

Special Characteristic #6: Multiple parentage and inter-familial consensual adoptions.

Consistent with the axiomatic contention of a continued African world-view operating within the cultural milieu of Euro (White)-American culture, we suggest that the Black family system should be thought of as African in "nature" and American in "nurture". The intrinsic nature or integrity of the Black family system is, therefore, African. This "integrity" of Black families, we have termed the sense of "Africanity". The Black family, consequently, can only be fully understood when it is conceived as a unit or system embedded in an Euro-American cultural milieu but which derives its primary characteristics, forms, and definitions from its African nature.

A proposed theoretical and empirical framework for defining Black families must, therefore, suggest the following:

Approach: The "Cultural Continuity" model contends that Black culture in the United States is the result of a special admixture of our continued African world-view or cultural perspective operating within an environment which is primarily defined by the cultural

perspectives of an Anglo-American world-view.
Axiom #1
An African cultural spectrum forms the foundation of the Black cultural sphere.
Axiom #2
Anglo-American culture serves as the medium in which the Black cultural spectrum must operate.
Research Assumption: It is the combined (1) continuation of the African value system and (2) its reaction to the cultural imperatives of the wider Anglo-American value system which form the root of the special features observable in Black family life.
Methodological Issues: In terms of the phenomena known as Black family systems, the logic of discovery must proceed in:

1) explicating the philosophical or cultural world-view which guides and defines the phenomena. This philosophy or world-view is the basis for, or the foundation of the family's nature or integrity;

2) developing a theoretical model and/or conceptualization which is consistent with the intrinsic philosophical world-view;

3) demonstrating the particular way in which that intrinsic world-view manifests itself and/or is affected by contemporary factors (i.e., racism, economics, etc.).
Corollary: There is diversity in Black families; however, within that diversity one is able to discern a comprehensive cultural theme which has historically characterized Black families. It is this cultural theme (screen) or commonality which we refer to as the sense of "Africanity".
Interpretive Ruling: The observable behavioral outcomes must be interpreted in terms of

understanding (1) the African nature or basis for the "behavior", and (2) the American conditions which influence their development and/or expression.

Theoretical Framework: Black families in America are African-based families.

Empirical Implications: (1) Black families must be viewed as contemporary extension of African family forms with identifiable modifications (usually due to racism, political and economic exploitation). (2) The re-interpretation of Black family life must be based on the retention of African cultural residuals as expressed in Black families.

This final point is extremely important because it is critical in relation to the issue of conceptual incarceration and transubstantive error. It also defines the model as an interactive model.

CHAPTER SEVEN

Implications and Applications of the Africanity Model

Chapter 7

Implications and Applications of the Africanity Model

The research on the Black family currently being conducted at the Institute for the Advanced Study of Black Family Life and Culture, Inc. is the continuation of The Black Family research programme which began at Westside Community Mental Health Center. The intent of the original research project was to re-investigate the nature of Black family systems. The results discussed below are based on data associated with the original study entitled, "A Formulative and Empirical Study of Black Families" (cf: Nobles, 1976a).

The proposal upon which this research was designed clearly indicated our intention to offer a conceptual description of contemporary Black family systems. Consequently, the primary goal of the study was to delineate and describe the guiding principles and/or philosophical basis of Black family life.

Consistent with the above discussions, we began this research with the belief or assumption that the acceptance of a continuous cultural theme was important to the development of an accurate reflective analysis of Black family life. As noted above, the cultural continuity approach to the study of

Black family systems contends that Black culture in the United States is the result of a special admixture of our continued African world-view or cultural perspective operating within an environment which is primarily defined by the cultural perspectives of Anglo-American society. Accordingly, we believe it is the African cultural spectrum which is at the base of the Black cultural sphere, while the Anglo-American spectrum serves as the medium in which the Black cultural spectrum must operate. Consequently, it is the combined continuation of the African value system and its reaction to the cultural imperatives of the wider, Anglo-American society which form the root of the special features observable in Black family life.

In documenting the features of the Black family system we analyzed the data in terms of the structural elements that comprise the family as a social institution. Four general systemic features were examined - organizational purpose, social organization, interpersonal relations and role relations. Organizational purpose refers to the primary purpose of being for the organization, its raison d'etre. Hence, it selects and determines what is of importance to the organization. By social organization we refer to the organized pattern of relations within the organization. In a general sense social organization refers to the ethos or set of guiding principles by which the organization operates and by which its members must abide. Interpersonal relations reflect the character of relations within the organized pattern. Role relations refer to the proper and/or customary functions of members of the organization.

These structural features in a sense would distinguish one cultural group from another in that they reflect a people's "general design for living and patterns for interpreting reality". In this sense, then, the nature of the family system represents, in microcosm and as a living organism, the cultural aspects of a people.

Organizational Purpose: In terms of the organizational purpose of the Black family, the family's reason for being can be considered childcenteredness. By this is meant that the purpose of the Black family focused on, if not required, the presence of children. The family unit exists for the affirmation of life. That is, it exists for the growth and development of children, rather than for the self-actualization of the adult members of the unit. The frequency of child-oriented or child-related comments and responses suggests that the informants were constantly taking into account the presence of their children, or children in general, when considering the general purpose of a family. In relation to this, our data revealed that storytelling was a means of transmitting a particular culture (i.e., language, values, rhythm, beliefs, and established traditions) to the young in Black families. Parenthetically, we must note that the live storytelling which the parents in our study experienced as children has been almost replaced by the television for their own children. In spite of the effects of television, however, our data show that Black parents still insist on teaching their children "humanistic" and "moralistic" values as opposed to competitive and individualistic values. Generally child-rearing practices in Black families are characterized by an atmosphere of family orientation and unconditional love which places a special emphasis on strong family ties, respect for elders and sees the child as possessing a natural goodness. Within this concept the child's feelings of competence are confirmed through his participation in household activities. In Black families children are socialized to assume significant responsibilities and express mature social behavior at a young age. On a cognitive level the responsibilities assumed within the household by Black children reinforce their own sense of self-worth and provide them with some appropriate practical skills to negotiate the adult world and the wider social system. In addition the socialization process in Black families employs, amongst other things, mutual aid, adaptability, interdependence, compassion, and a strong obligation toward familial and non-familial networks in the community.

Social Organization: One of the most striking findings of this research is that in spite of the extreme urbanism and metropolitan isolation of San Francisco, the Black families in this study revealed a close network of relationships within and between families not necessarily related by blood. This "family networking" in the Black community, though being seriously eroded by the imperatives of urban life, has served as an unrecognized cohesive force in the community and has been the basis of many services (i.e., child-care, financial aid, counseling) which are otherwise unavailable to Black people. The special aspect of the "family networking" worth highlighting is the "elastic" nature of the family structurally. Our data suggest that the Black family, essentially, stretches to accommodate new members (i.e., non-blood relatives) into the network. The importance of these "social relatives" and/or para-kin is almost indistinguishable from biological and/or legal relatives. The close intra-family as well as the cohesive inter-family network serves both pragmatic and/or psychological functions. Structurally, the Black family is a living organism that stretches and diminishes in response to external conditions that impact on it. Thus at any one time in its cycle of expansion and contraction the family will take a different form. This indicates that there is no one type or kind of Black family and that at any time in its history the family unit can have a different structure.

It is understandable that families which reflect the "family networking" concept would also express the importance (often times, equal importance) of persons, other than the biological parents, in the lives of the children. Our data indicated that Black parents were not, for instance, the sole agents of value transmission to their young. The analyses suggest that in terms of the social organization of Black families, its functions and structures are primarily inclusive and elastic, respectively.

One could, however, argue, as many have (cf: Adams, 1970), that the "family networking" is nothing but the result of kinship ties created out of the necessary

poverty. That is to say, the particular pattern of
kinship ties are pre-requisites to survival for
minority status groups in a hostile society; and
the fact of wide-spread hostility simply
strengthened and expanded Black kin ties.
The obvious transubstantive error, of course, is
the interpretation of Black kinship ties as a
response akin to "we either hang together or
hang alone". The Africanity framework would
recognize the family networking phenomenon
and interpret it as a response stemming from
(1) the retention of an African cultural attitude
which reflects the Oneness of Being and the
notion of Interdependence, and (2) a response
to White American hostility. Parenthetically,
the value of this system is heightened by the
hostility characteristic of White American
society. The observable behavioral outcome
(i.e., family networking) is interpreted in
terms of understanding the African nature
(Oneness of Being and Interconnectedness)
and the American conditions (racism and
hostility toward Blacks).

Interpersonal Relations: It is probably true
that the interpersonal relationships
characterizing a family are directly related to
the family's particular definition of its social
organization and organizational purpose.
Clearly, the principles by which the family
guides its activities and the parameters which
define its integrity influence the way in which
the family acts internally. The data suggest
that the Black family is comprised of several
individual households with the family
definition and lines of authority and decision-
making transcending any one household unit
which comprises the "family". That is,

decisions affecting the lives of members of one household may be made in a different household that represented the "seat of authority" for that family.   In terms of interpersonal relationships, one of the most striking qualities of Black family life was the presence of "multiple parentage".   Our data clearly indicated, in various ways, that the families in our study received help in rearing their children from other members of the family.   In this context older siblings perform significant child-rearing functions in the Black family.   In addition parents reported in this study that it was not unusual for their children to be allowed to visit other relatives and sometimes, to stay with those relatives for relatively long periods of time as "members" of their relatives' immediate households.   These temporary and/or periodic "interfamilial consensual adoptions" must have a real profound effect on the child's development. The recognition and respect for several "parents" or "multiple parents", may, for instance, be related to the child's sense of "generalized authority", or better still, "relative authority" as a function of time and space.   Psychologically, children are able to identify and interact with several adults.   One clear consequence of "multiple parentage" is that children have early exposure to the varied and complex aspects of adult types, behaviors and responsibilities.   They are exposed to several types of roles and role performances. In terms of roles, the ensuing role flexibility characteristic of many Black family dynamics essentially provides or prepares the child, regardless of sex, to deal with the requirements of many different situations, tasks, and functions. Another consequence may be the child's requisite need to understand the basis of one's authority (i.e., family bond) prior to submission or obedience to that authority.

Again, the consideration of the African world-view (Oneness of Being and Notion of Interconnectedness) provides the African framework with explanative power. The retention of a cultural attitude which recognizes the nature of all things as the Supreme Force and the interconnectedness of all elements would influence one's interpersonal relations. Specifically, such a retention would allow one to "see" as appropriate respect for all adults, ergo, "multiple parents". Similarly, such a world-view would also allow one to "see" as normal the inter-familial consensual adoptions. This latter feature, though consistent with the cultural fabric of African peoples, is simultaneously, a response which many could view as stemming from the hardship of American society. As an observable behavioral outcome, it (inter-familial consensual adoptions) could be interpreted as evidence of the weakness of the "family bond". This, of course, would be a transubstantive error. Traditionally, Africans viewed every adult as responsible for all the children. Therefore, it would not matter which adult at any given moment was given the custody of a particular child. The retention of this attitude was probably the mechanism which historically made informal adoptions in Black communities work.

The nature of the interpersonal relationships in the family may very well be the basis of interpersonal relationships on a wider scale. It clearly is reflected in role performance. The ease and/or difficulty experienced by members of Black families may be found in the disparity between the nature of their families and the nature of the wider society.

Role Relations: As noted previously, children in Black families are exposed to several types of roles (both in and outside of their immediate households). Role relations within the Black family are flexible and interchangeable. In terms of intentional or specific roles, parents in our study made a clear distinction between "definition" and "performance". On the one hand, they spoke of role definition in sex-linked terms. On the other hand, they discussed role performance without regard to sex. Our data indicate, for instance, that parents felt it very important for their male children to learn what it means to be masculine and possess manly qualities; while, for their female children, the emphasis was placed on understanding and acquiring feminine qualities. In both instances, the responses were very clearly in relation to "definition" and not necessarily "performance". The data on role performance overwhelmingly attest to the position of Black parents that their children, regardless of sex, should be equipped with the pragmatic skills and psychological attitudes to support themselves and their families.

Though the opinion of the wider society focuses on the uselessness and burden of the elderly, our research suggests that in Black families, the elderly still have a viable and important role to play in the affairs of family life. One such aspect, which is so evident we often take it for granted, is that the elderly are the carriers of the largest amount of information on family heritage and the repositories of the longest living history. Our research revealed that the elderly were most often the storytellers in the families. Hence, they served the critical function of instilling in the young, via storytelling, a sense of family. The elderly were also a critical source of psychological support in easing the traumas of family transitions and/or crises.

In general, the performance of various roles and the expression of certain role definitions were always in response to the needs of the family. The responses of our informants suggest that the performance of any role and/or the definition of any individual's role was deemed appropriate and/or inappropriate as a consequence of its meaning to the viability and/or goals of the family.

In terms of observable behavioral outcomes (i.e., role flexibility), the typical transubstantive error has been to assume a relationship between role performance/role models and personality disposition. This, of course, is the crux of most of the absent parent research. The real effect, given the Africanity model and its assumptions of role performance and role models, as well as any phenomena associated with Black family life, has to be determined and/or interpreted in terms of the African-based cultural perspective, normative assumptions, and frame of reference.

The analysis of the structural features of the Black family reveals a system that is primarily inclusive, responsive and interconnected. It is clear that these features of the Black family derive from, and are consistent with, the African ontological and cosmological understanding of the universe. Through its features the Black family system is reflective of a cultural orientation that sees everything as being of the same substance (the principle of family networking, multiple parentage, interfamilial consensual adoption) and being interconnected (role flexibility, family elasticity, role responsibility).

The utility of the model in this analysis is that it allows us to see that while some of the features of the Black family may be attributed to some of the concrete conditions, the underlying dimensions of the family system emerge from the cultural basis.

CONCLUSION

There is an African proverb that says, "when a fool fails to turn Ebony White, he tries to Blacken ivory". The state of Black family life in America, ultimately may be captured in this proverb. Scientific research and social services programs alike have historically been the "fool" attempting to Whiten the ebony of Black family dynamics. We clearly are at a junction wherein our next response will determine if Black families change into White families (as the proverb predicts), or if White social science begins the task of trying to prove how White families should be more like Black families, naturally, without calling themselves such.

For us, we contend, the change from "Black" to "White" is too costly. It amounts to the sacrifice of our children's humaneness. For "ebony" to become "ivory", we and our children must give up the sense of struggle, the sense of righteousness, the sense of commitment and the sense of "we-ness". We must become individually self-centered and concerned with only our personal well-being and development. This, we, in all honesty, recognize to be happening right now. The intensive contact with White people, primarily through the electronic media, is taking its toll and the issue of "people survival" is rapidly waning in the wake of "I've got to do my own thing". In so doing, the Black family faces a loss of its "humanism" for a new "individualism".

We, Black social scientists particularly, but Black people in general, therefore, have a choice. The choice is to consciously begin to reinforce the historical sense of Blackness and humanism in our people, or allow the effects of Americanization (via schools, the media, etc.) to convince us that our "ebony is White". To allow for the latter is to participate in the destruction of our own families. To do such is to remain the victim of the legacy and to continue the lie. To choose the former is to set the stage for accurate reflective analysis of Black psycho-cultural reality. To choose the former, in brief, is to struggle for the survival of our humaneness. The choice, of liberation or continued oppression is ours. If liberation struggles are, by definition, struggles to reclaim the right of culture (i.e., the right of an indigenous vast structure of language, behavior, customs, knowledge, symbols, ideas, and values which influence the general design for living and patterns for interpreting reality), then liberation struggles must develop and utilize a science of their own making (as science of their own culture).   It is in the reclamation of culture and in the creative reconstruction of it as science that one seizes control over the interpretation of reality; and, consequently, connects struggle with human development.   As the expression of all that constitutes the everyday way of life of a people, culture defines and gives meaning to everything experienced by the living. Accordingly, culture defines and gives meaning to the notion of human development; and, science, as its reconstruction, simply further refines the definition and meaning of that human development.

As a reconstruction of the systematic and cumulative ideas, beliefs and knowledge (i.e., common sense) of a people, science's role in liberation struggles, therefore, must be to further filter, organize and transform "sensations" into particular mental impressions and behavioral dispositions and/or responses.

The role of Black social science must, therefore, be to provide the arena for (1) the reclamation of the right of culture, and (2) the reconstruction of reality (science).   In so doing, Black social science will provide a redefinition of our concrete condition and thereby provide the mechanism for expressing and defining New World Africans' capacity to create progress and determine history.

Footnotes

Footnotes

1. Blacks associated with the planning group included : Martin Kilson; Kenneth Clark; Whitney Young; Ralph Ellison; G. Franklin Edwards; John Hope Franklin; St. Clair Drake and Adelaide Cromwell Hill; Whites on the planning group included: Everett C. Hughes; Philip M. Hauser; Erik Erikson; Talcott Parsons; Lee Rainwater; James O. Wilson; Oscar Handlin and Daniel P. Moynihan. (This represents only a partial listing).

2. Hare identifies Andrew Billingsley, Joyce Ladner, Robert Staples and Nobles as "leaders" in this school of thought. The one person who unashamedly discussed strengths in Black families, Robert Hill, is not mentioned. Personally, the work associated with Nobles, i.e., the Africanity Model, has never been offered as a strengths approach to the study of Black family life. In this case, Hare misunderstood the thrust and position of the research.

3. Developments in mechanics (physics) paralleled and assisted techniques in architecture and military arts; advances in biology were in direct response to problems in the areas of animal husbandry and human health, while those in chemistry seemed to respond to the developing fields of iron and dyeing industries.

4. Ideology is never absent. It may not take

the form of an organized expression; however, it is always present.

5. In this case, socialization refers to the internalization to (as one's own) the "meaning" of that group's primary definition.

6. This does not mean we do not take into account White reality, it means where White reality is relevant we define it from a Black perspective.

7. In order to be conceptually correct, one should not, however, separately discuss cosmology and ontology.

8. For Black people, however, our socialization process has taken on a new function. Given the racist hostility and continued oppression by the wider Anglo-American cultural community, Black culture has taken on the special functions (or, at least this particular role of culture was intensified) of protecting Black people from the devastating effects of the dominant social reality, i.e., racism. That is, Black culture as expressed in the many and varied agencies (i.e., the church, the family, etc.) in the Black community historically provided Black people with a "buffer" which blocked most (though, clearly not all) of the negative oppression directed at Black people.

9. When the psychologists or social scientists are all alike or similar in their world views, e.g., APA, then the influence or professional association is probably compounded by the common world view.

Glossary

Glossary

Argument
Any discourse, dialog or discussion which has a "statement of reason" and "transference of belief" is considered in western logic to be an argument.

Axiology
A component of the cultural factor level which pertains to a people's assumptions or beliefs about the primary characteristics of universal relationships.

Common Sense
Common sense pertains to the recognition that knowing results in part from the human ability to be aware of (sense) reality and that there are aspects of this sensory process which characterize and are common to a particular group of people. Hence, common sense pertains to awareness which is characteristic of the total group's knowing of reality.

Conceptual Incarceration
Conceptual incarceration is the highest or most   sophisticated   level   of   scientific colonialism. It is the process whereby alien ideas or concepts are utilized to explain and/or understand the reality of a particular people. The utilization of alien concepts results in the knower being limited in what he can know about the phenomenon under study.

Constructionist Response
The constructionist response is an intellectual response which attempts to create from the cultural prerequisites of African people a basic

and authentic body of information and ideas.

Cosmology

Cosmology is a component of the cultural factor which pertains to a people's assumptions or beliefs about the origin and the structure of reality (universe).

Culture

Culture is a process which gives a people a general design for living and patterns for interpreting their reality. The model of culture provided in this text consists of three levels : (1) cultural aspects; (2) cultural factors ; and (3) cultural manifestations.

Cultural Aspects

The cultural aspects are comprised of : (1) ideology; (2) ethos; and (3) world-view.

Cultural Factors

The cultural factors are comprised of : (1) ontology; (2) cosmology; and (3) axiology.

Cultural Manifestations

The cultural manifestations are the overt expressions of a people's culture. It consists of behavior, values and attitudes, etc.

Cultural Prerequisites

Cultural prerequisites are those processes, functions and/or attributes which emerge from a people's "sense of being" and which must be protected in order to guarantee their cultural identity.

Cultural Substance

Cultural substance is a term used to connote the "aspect" and "factor" levels of the cultural model. Its importance is that the cultural substance gives "meaning" to the overt manifestations of a people's culture (i. e., their human conduct) .

Deconstructionist Response
The deconstructionist response is an intellectual response wherein the purpose is to expose the error, weakness and/or irrelevance of western scientific information to Black reality. In effect its purpose is to tear down the false edifice of western science.

Dialectic
Discussion and reasoning by dialogue as a method of intellectual investigation, development through the stages of thesis, antithesis and synthesis in accordance with the laws of dialectical materialism.

Empiricism
This is a method of knowing based on the belief that knowledge is acquired by observation since a phenomenon (reality) is measurable by the senses and locatable in time and space.

Epistemology
In the philosophy of science, epistemology is a focus which pertains to the study of the nature and grounds of knowledge or knowing and what is considered real especially with reference to its limits and validity.

Epistemological Chain
This symbolically represents the connection between "observation", "assumption", "question", "method", "answer", "prescription" and "new observation". The term pertains to the recognition that just as the nature of the question influences the realm in which the answer will fall so too are the types of questions influenced by the culture of the questioner. These components of knowing are linked together in a chain of influence.

Ethos
A people's ethos is the tone, character, and quality of their life, its moral and aesthetic style and mode. It emerges as a set of guiding principles which define the underlying attitude they have toward themselves and their world.

Existential
Having being in time and space, grounded in existence or the experience of existence.

Human Imperatives
Human imperatives are those processes and functions which must be performed in order for a people to continue as a group irrespective of cultural form.

Hypothesis
A hypothesis is a guess about the "functional relationship" between an antecedent (cause) condition and a consequent (effect) condition which can be tested by observation and/or experimentation.

Ideology
Ideology is essentially a concept representing the instrument which provides a critique of reality. It determines how a people should see their reality; and, in so doing, influences (possibly dictates) the nature of a people's awareness (consciousness). Ideology serves as the "map" which clarifies and gives perspective to problematic aspects of a people's social reality.

Integrated Modificationism
Integrated modificationism is an intermediate level of scientific colonialism whereby information and/or ideas are intentionally distorted, fabricated and/or made deceptive in order to influence the process of knowing.

Law
In science a law is a statement that relates one set on antecedent facts (independent variables) to at least one other set of consequent facts (dependent variables).

Metaphysics
The study of the nature and structure of being (ontology) and of the origin and general structure of the universe (cosmology). It is also considered a theory or system concerning ontology and cosmology. (Some philosophers use this term simply as a synonym for ontology, excluding cosmology. Others use it pejoratively as a synonym for "nonsense").

Methodology
This is the agreed upon convention which serves as the system(s) of proofs and measurements of reality. It is the method by which knowledge and information is acquired and scientific theory protected.

Nomological Deductive Reasoning
This is a method wherein it is assumed that : (1) events are nameable, observable, related and predictable; and (2) one can deduce a "truth" about one named phenomenon from another (named) known phenomenon.

Ontology
Ontology is a component of the cultural factor level which pertains to a people's assumptions or beliefs about the nature of existence or the essence of being.

Paralyzed Intellectual
A paralyzed intellectual is one whose critical thinking does not benefit from responding to Blackness or Africanity as a central component in the analytical framework.

Phenomenalism
The view that the reality of a material object consists in its being perceived by some perceiver with the corollary that the physical world does not exist apart from the actual or possible perceptions of some perceiver, i.e., subjective idealism.

Philosophy
The original synthesis of knowledge; the attitude to the world and to life's problems; the elaboration, often implicit and more confusedly felt than clearly expressed, of a cosmology.

Power
Power is the ability to define reality and have other people respond to your definition as if it were their own.

Pulled Intellectual
A pulled intellectual is one whose critical thinking is determined by, or motivated in relation to, the need to explicate the intrinsic nature of Blackness. In effect, the pulled intellectual is one who is responding to the need to produce information designed to recognize and build upon the uniqueness of Black culture.

Pushed Intellectual
A pushed intellectual is one whose critical thinking is determined by, or motivated in relation to, the prevailing intellectual atmosphere. In effect the pushed intellectual is one who is reacting to the information and ideas found in the wider intellectual community. This reaction is generally an attempt to refute the negative image and demonstrate the worthiness of Black people.

Rationalism
Rationalism is a method of knowing based on the belief that reality can be understood by the manipulation of ideas and that knowledge is acquired by "reasoning".

Reason
In western logic a reason is any statement cited to: (1) support; (2) explain; or (3) justify some further statement of claim, expectation or assertion.

Reasoning
In western logic this pertains to an analytical method involving movement in thought from an already known "truth" or true statement to a further (unrecognized) "truth" or true statement.

Reconstructionist Response
The reconstructionist response is an intellectual response wherein the purpose is to correct the error of western science and to "reconstruct" more sensitive and relevant models, theories and applications.

Science
Science is thought to be a systematic, regulated process for acquiring substantiated and valid information which is generally characterized by (1) a method for organizing and explaining reality; (2) a set of procedures for amplifying and specifying the common sense of a people; and (3) the development of models whereby one reconstructs reality.

Scientific Colonialism
Scientific colonialism is a term utilized to connote that science as a process in human relations qualifies in its treatment of African and African-American phenomena as a colonial exploitative system. Any system of

relationships which are characterized by : (1) removal of wealth; (2) claim to the right of access; and (3) an external power base, qualifies as a colonial relationship. When the scientific process satisfies these three conditions it is scientific colonialism. Under the process of scientific colonialism, knowledge and information are rigidly controlled by the methodology or mechanisms of destruction, distortions, fabrications, and suppression.

Scientific Fact
A scientific fact is nothing more than an agreed upon observation.

Theory
A theory is a statement or set of statements that relate functionally at least two sets of laws. Essentially a theory differs from a law only in its scope and its generality. Simplistically, a theory is a symbolic representation of a people's practice.

Transference of Belief
This is a process whereby belief in one statement leads to (is transferred to) a belief in a "connected" statement.

Transubstantiation
Transubstantiation is a process whereby the "cultural substance" of one group of people is utilized to give "meaning" to the cultural manifestations of another group of people.

Transubstantive Errors
Transubstantive errors are literally "mistakes of meaning". They occur when the cultural manifestations of two groups of people are similar, yet the cultural substance, which gives the manifestations meaning, is different. The knower of one culture will attribute meaning,

for instance, to behavior of a member of another culture utilizing his/her own cultural substance. To the extent that the cultural substance of the two groups differs, the knower will erroneously interpret the behavior in terms of his/her own perspective and thereby commit a transubstantive error.

Unsophisticated Falsification

This is a procedure where information and/or ideas are destroyed and/or suppressed and falsified in order to influence the process of knowing. It is the lowest level of scientific colonialism.

World-view

A people's world-view is their picture of the way things in sheer actuality are, their concept of nature, of self, of society. It contains their most comprehensive ideas of order.

Bibliography

Bibliography

ADAMS, P.L. Functions of the lower-class partial families. *American Journal of Psychiatry,* 130, 2: 223-241, 1973.

ALDOUS, J. Wife's employment status and lower class men as husbands: Support for Moynihan thesis. *Journal of Marriage and the Family,* 31, 469-476, 1969.

BERNARD, J. *Marriage and family amongst negroes.* Prentice-Hall, Inc.: Englewood Cliffs, New Jersey, 1966.

BILLINGSLEY, A. *Black families in White America,* Prentice-Hall, Inc.: Englewood Cliffs, New Jersey, 1968.

CABRAL, A. *Return to the source: Selected speeches of Amilcar Cabral.* New York: Monthly Review Press, 1973.

CHILMAN, N.C. *Growing up poor.* U.S. Department of Health, Education and Welfare, 1966.

CLARK, C.C. Black studies or the study of Black people. In Reginald Jones (Ed.), *Black Psychology,* New York: Harper and Row, Inc. 1972.

DELANY, M.R. *The condition, elevation, emigration, and destiny of the colored people of the United States.* New York: Arno Press, 1969.

FRAZIER, E.F. *The negro family in Chicago.* Chicago: The University of Chicago press, 1932.

FRAZIER, E.F. *The negro family in the United States.* Chicago: The University of Chicago Press, 1939.

HALL, G. S. The negro in Africa and America. *Pedagogical Seminary* 12, 350-368, 1905.

HARE, N. What Black intellectuals misunderstood about the Black family. *Black World*, 20, 4-14, 1976.

HILL, R.B. *The strength of Black families.* New York: Harper and Row, 1972.

JEFFERS, C. *Living poor.* Ann Arbor, Michigan: Ann Arbor Publishers, 1967.

JONES, M. Scientific methods as a tool for improving the quality of value judgement with particular concern for the Black predicament in the United States. *The Review of Black Political Economy 7* (Fall): 7-21. 1976.

KARENGA, M. *Essays on struggle: Position and analysis.* San Diego: Kawaida Publications, 1978.

KUHN, T. *The structure of scientific revolutions.* Chicago: Chicago University Press, 1963.

LADNER, J. A. *Tomorrow's tomorrow: The Black woman.* Garden City, New York: Anchor, 1972.

LIEBOW, E. *Tally's corner.* Boston: Little, Brown and Company. 1967.

LYNCH, H.R. (ed.) *Black spokesman: Selected published writings of Edward Wilmot Blyden.* London: Frank Cass and Co. Ltd., 1971.

MANNHEIM, K. *Ideology and utopia.* New York: Harcourt, Brace and World, 1936.

MBITI, J.S. *African religions and philosophy.* New York: Anchor Books. 1970.

MERTON, ROBERT K. *The sociology of science*. Chicago: The University of Chicago Press.

MOYNIHAN, D.P. *The Negro family: The case for national action.* Washington, D.C.: U.S. Department of Labor, Office of Planning and Research, 1965.

NAGEL, E. *The structure of science.* New York: Harcourt, Brace and World, Inc.

NOBLES, W.W. African root and American fruit: The Black family. *Journal of Social and Behavioral Sciences*, Winter, 1974a.

NOBLES, W.W. Africanity: Its role in Black families. *The Black Scholar,* 5 no. 9, 1974b.

NOBLES, W.W. A formulative and empirical study of Black families. DHEW Publication (OCD-90-C-255). Washington, D.C.: Office of Child Development, Department of Health, Education and Welfare, 1976a.

NOBLES, W.W. Toward a reflective analysis of Black families: The absence of a grounding (or how do you know what you know?), Paper presented at Invitational Symposium, Atlanta University School of Social Work, Atlanta, Georgia, June. 1976b.

NOBLES, W.W. & GODDARD, L.L. *Understanding the Black family: A guide to scholarship and research.* Oakland, Calif: Black Family Institute Publishers, 1984.

OSEI, G.K. *The African philosophy of life.* London: The African Publication Society. 1970.

RAINWATER, L. *Behind ghetto walls: Negro families in a federal slum.* Chicago: Aldine Publishing Company. 1970.

RODMAN, H. *Lower-class value stretch.* Social Change 4 (December): 205-215. 1963.

SCANZONI, J. *The Black family in modern society*, Boston: Alyn and Beachum. 1970.

STAPLES, R. Toward a sociology of the Black family: A decade of theory and research, *Journal of Marriage and Family*, 33, 19-38, 1971.

STAPLES, R. The Black family revisited: A review and preview, *Journal of Social and Behavioral Sciences*, 24, 1974.

TEMPELS, P. Bantu philosophy. Paris: *Presence' Africaine*. 1959.

TERMAN, L. *The measurement of intelligence.* Cambridge, Mass: Riverside Press, 1916.

THOMAS, L.V. A Senegalese philosophical system: The cosmology of the Jolah people. *Presence' Africaine* 4-5 (32-33): 192-203. 1960.

THOMAS, L.V. Time, myth and history in West Africa. *Presence' Africaine* 11 (39):50-92. 1961.

THORNDIKE, E. L. *Human nature and the social order.* New York: MacMillan, 1940.

VON LUE, T. Transubstantiation in the study of African reality. *African Affairs* 74 (October): 401-419. 1975.

WILLIE, C. *The family life of Black people.* Columbus, Ohio: Charles E. Merrill Books. 1970.

Author's Index

Author's Index

Subject Index

Subject Index

The Institute makes available its materials in a variety of forms including educational video cassettes, audio tapes, research reports, research and policy highlights and reprints of publications. For further information on this publication and the other scholarly materials of the Institute please contact :
William E. Cavil, III
Associate Director
Development and Dissemination
Institute for the Advanced Study of
Black Family Life and Culture, Inc.
P. O. Box 24739
Oakland, Ca. 94623